AF673831

INDIAN NATIONALISM AND TILAK

Indian Nationalism and Tilak: A Critical Analysis

ARTI

NATIONAL book ORGANISATION
(PUBLISHERS—DISTRIBUTORS)

Indian Nationalism and Tilak: A Critical Analysis

First published 1999

© Author

Published by

National Book Organisation
(Publishers–Distributors)
H-39, Green Park Extension
New Delhi-110016 (INDIA)

Mrs. A.H. Marwah–Publisher

ISBN 81-85135-99-1

Dedicated to

LORD GAURISHANKAR
The Supreme blessed of my late grandfather
Shri Paras Nath Singh whose ideals are the
torch-bearer of my life.

and

SHRI JANAKIVALLABHA
The supreme blessed of my lovely grandmother
Smt. Sita Devi Singh.

Contents

Preface

I am glad to have a chance for analysing the various aspects of nationalistic ideas of Lokmanya Bal Gangadhar Tilak through this book and comparing it with the modern national outlook.

Tilak having a great knowledge of Sanskrit, Mathematics, Astrology, Law and English sacrificed his whole life to the freedom movement of India. He was above all a great patriot.

Tilak linked the concept of 'Swaraj' with the Gita ideal of 'Karmayoga'. He wanted to substantiate the nationalistic movement in India by a strong cultural and religious revival of Hinduism. He started the two festivals, viz., Ganapati and Shivaji festivals, for this purpose. He was a bitter enemy of British bureacracy and wanted to remove it at any cost.

Tilak was a hard social worker. His services during the famine and plague will be always be memorable. He was alos conscious of other social problems, such as Sarda Sadan Vivad and the Wogvars' problem.

Tilak was not an Internationalist but was far from narrow nationalism. His memorandum to the Paris Peace Conference can be regarded as the first document of the present foreign policy of India.

As far as this work is concerned I have no word of thanks for Dr. L.N. Sharma, University Professor, Patna University, for his constant encouragement and guidance. I am also thankful to Dr. V.P. Verma, Ex-Head of the Department, Political Science, Patna University, for his precious advice and cooperation. Thanks go to also Mr. Rajesh Raj, Research Officer, Australian National University, Canberra, with whom I made useful discussions of different aspects of Nationalism. I am thankful to Mr. Jyoti Kumar also for his help.

I am thankful to the members of the staff of S.N. Sinha Library, Patna, A.N. Sinha Institute, Library, Patna and the Departmental Library of Political Science Department, Patna University for their cooperation.

Finally I bow my head to the kindness of the Almighty and pay my gratitute to the blessings of my parents and elders, which gave strength to my acton.

Acknowledgement

The present work on "Indian Nationalism and Tilak: A Critical Analysis:, is the result of hard work done during the last six years.

This work has become possible due to the able guidance of my respected supervisor, Dr. L.N. Sharma, to whom I can pay only my high sense of gratitute.

I am also deeply thankful to Dr. V.P. Verma (Ex. Head of the Deptt. Pol. Sc., Patna University) for his precious advice and cooperation. I am thankful to Dr. Mrs. prabhawati Sinha, Head, Deptt. of Political Science for her constant encouragement. I also express my thanks to Mr. Rajesh Raj, now Research Officer, Australian National University, Canberra, with whom I made useful discussions on different aspects of nationalism. I am also thankful to Mr. Jyoti Kumar and Mrs. Rashmi Sinha for their cooperation.

I am also thankful to the members of the staff of S.N. Sinha Library, Patna, A.N. Sinha Institute library, Patna University Library and the Departmental Library of Political Science Department, Patna University, for their cooperation.

Finally, I bow my head to the kindness of the Almighty and pay my gratitute to the blessings of my respected parents and elders, which gave strength to my action.

ARTI

1 Introduction

The nature of country's nationalism is in the main the outcome of interaction between a country's history and tradition and the demands of social change and modernization. But in the long run, it becomes important as to which between the two variables of tradition and modernity influences more, in what degree and to what extent. For example, in modern India, democracy, socialism and secularism characterize our nation - and state-building efforts. But it is important to examine whether these values were cherished by leaders like Bal Gangadhar Tilak who dominated the Pre-Gandhian phase of Indian nationalism and paved the path for the mass movement for Indian independence to begin. The broad aim of this research project is to examine the nature and basis of nationalism in India keeping Tilak's concept of nationalism as the central focus for comparison and evaluation.

Origin and Basis of Indian Nationalism

The concept of nation-state trimphed in Europe in the fifteenth century. But the subjugated nations of Asia and Africa seethed with the aspiration to gain the status of a nation-state during the latter half of the nineteenth and the earlier part of the twentieth century. In Europe, Hegel and others expounded the concept of nationalism; whereas in India, Aurobindo, Tilak and others expounded it. A striking feature of Indian nationalism is that neither its pioneer nor subsequent leaders evolved or accepted the materialist philosophy.[1] Not only Haeckel, Feurbach and Marx were thoroughgoing materialists, Kant and Spencer, too, were agnostic and Hume was a sceptic. In contrast, all leaders of Indian nationalism in the philosophical, political or cultural field, such as Ram Mohan Roy, Gokhale, Tilak, Banerjee, Pal, Aurobindo, Lala Lajpat Rai, Tagore, Gandhi, Abul Kalam Azad, Iqbal, J.C. Bose and others stood for religious reform in different ways and varying degrees. But none of them challenged or repudiated religion or the idea of God on which religion was based.

The non-materialist conception of Indian nationalism owes its origin to the fact that Indian nationalism developed in a peculiar way. Modern materialism was an integral, though a very small functional part of the total European culture. Since this culture happened to be the culture of the British who had conquered and dominated India, the nationalist leaders felt a conscious or subconscious recoil from it. Whereas they copied the parliamentary structure; in the sphere of philosophy, they felt that India must stand on its own legs and must draw from the philosophical legacy of the past, which was essentially religio-spiritual. This is, perhaps, one of the principal reasons why these leaders shunned modern materialism and even thoroughgoing rationalism. Raja Ram Mohan Roy in spite of his rationalist approach could not overcome his belief in the divinity of the Vedas. His successor, Devendranath Tagore, endeavoured to achieve a synthesis of reason and intuition. Keshab Chandra Sen proclaimed himself as a prophet entrusted with messages from God to be delivered to humanity. Pal and Aurobindo subscribed to the cult of spiritual mysticism. Lajpat Rai, the Arya Samajist, divinized the Veda. At a later stage, Gandhi, too, involed 'the inner voice' when he was confronted with a complicated political or social problem.[2] Tilak who pioneered political nationalism did not free himself from the tradition consciously. He reinterpreted the Gita and declared action to be its central teaching. The very kernel of the Gita's philosohy, he said, was missed by the Indian people who had, as a result, sunk into inertia and fatalistic moods. The Indian nation could be roused to dynamism only if they recognized this[3] and broke their bonds.

Growth of Indian Nationalism

Indian nationalism came into being during the British period as a result of the action and interaction of numerous other subjective and objective forces and factors which developed within the Indian society under the conditions of British rule and the impact of world forces.[4] It passed through various phases of development. As it advanced from one phase to another, its social basis broadened, its objective became more clearly defined and bold, and its forms of expression more varied. As a result of the impact of forces of Indian and world development, increasing strata of the Indian people evolved a national consciousness and outlook and were drawn into the orbit of the nationalist movement. This national awakening found expression in varied spheres of national life, social, political, cultural.[5]

These varied spheres were contributory to each other. Social, cultural and economic nationalism paved the path for political nationalism to grow and become stronger. The different streams have interlink among themselves, but in order to delineate the arrival of political nationalism, it is necessary to understand other spheres or phases of nationalism preceding it.

(A)Social Basis of Indian Nationalism

Raja Ram Mohan Roy and his group of enlightened Indians were the founders of social basis of Indian nationalism. They were exponents of the concept of the Indian nation which they propagated among the people. They initiated socio-reform and religio-reform movements which represented endeavours to remould the Indian society and religion in the spirit of the new principles of democracy, rationalism and nationalism. These founders and first fighters of Indian nationalism stood up for democratic rights, such as the freedom of the Press and put forth demands like the right of the nation to have a voice in the administration of the country.[6]

As facts stand, Ram Mohan Roy's break with traditions was deeply contradictory, accommodating within the same corpus of thinking numerous compromises with orthodoxy, Hindu elitist and by his own enligthtened standard clearly irrational way of thought and practice and in any case it was a break only on the intellectual plane and not at the level of basic social transformation.[7] In this economic thinking also, he accepted in toto the then fashionable logic of trade and seemed to visualize a kind of dependent but still real bourgeois development in Bengal in close collaboration with British merchants and entrepreneurs. This was an utterly absurd illusion, because colonial subjection would never permit full-blooded bourgeois modernity but only a weak and distorted caricature.[8]

Ishwar Chandra Vidyasagar was another 19th century social reformer of Bengal. Vidyasagar's own attempt at social reform, for instance, placed great reliance upon liberal backing by the colonial government. The failure of these attempts showed that his hopes were misplaced. He did not find any effective support for his schemes from within his own class. When arguing for reform, Vidyasagar, despite his own professed disregard for the sanctity or reasonableness of the shastra, felt compelled to look for scriptural support for his programmes. He did not think it feasible to attempt to create a nonconformism outside the bond of canonical orthodoxy. In fact, this remained a major ideological anomaly in all 19th century attempts to 'modernize' religion and social practice — a spurious conciliation of Indian idealism and imported liberal sanctions — which led to a major backlash after 1880 in the form of movement to revive traditional movements that were openly hostile to the earlier decades of reason and enlightenment.[9]

The 19th century intelligensia may have genuinely welcomed the new ideas of reason and rationality and some may even have shown considerable courage and enterprise in seeking to 'modernize' social customs and attitudes. But the fundamental forces of transformation were absent in colonial society. As a result, there was no possibility for the emergence of a consistently rational set of beliefs or practices. Liberalism stood on highly fragile foundations: reason dwindled to merely individual means of self-gratification without social responsibility.[10] While there were elements of modernity in the new cultural and intellectual movements in 19th century India, these could not become meaningful unless they were located, in their relation, to the changing socio-economic structure of the country, and on the other to the crucial context of power.[11]

(B) Economic Basis of Indian Nationalism

With social nationalism economic nationalism was framing its shape under the able leadership of the grand old soldier of Indian nationalism, Dadabhai Naoroji. According to him, the most important reason of the poverty in India was the 'drain' of wealth to England. The task was systematically undertaken by Dadabhai Naoroji with his characteristic statistical approach. He first referred to 'drain' in March 1866. By May 1867 a tentative draft of his thesis was redy.[12] In his paper, 'England's Debt to India', which Naoroji read before a meeting of East India Association London, on 2nd May 1867, he first put forward the idea that Britain was extracting wealth from India as the price of there rule in India, that out of revenues raised in India, nearly one-fourth goes clean out of the country, and is added to the resources of England and that India was consequently being continuously bled.[13] By 1873, when he prepared the first draft of his famous paper on 'Poverty of India', Dadabhai's views on the drain were beginning to be formulated in their more well-known militant form. By 1876, the drain theory had fully crystallised inhis mind and was presented in its entirety, in a revised draft of the 'Poverty of India', before the Bombay Branch of East India Association. From now, Dadabhai literally dedicated his life to propagation of the drain theory and to launching a roaring and raging campaign against the drain which was declared by him to be the fundamental evil of British rule in India.[14]

Many other Indian leaders, including G.V. Joshi, P.C. Ray, Madan Mohan Malaviya, D.E. Wacha, G.K. Gokhale, G.Subramaniya Iyar, Surendranath Banerjee and R.C. Dutt, joined in one stream of agitation around the question of drain. Justice Ranade delivered in 1872 a lecture at Poona on Indian trade and industry in which he criticised the drain of capital and resources from India and observed that of the national income of India more than one-third was taken away by the British in some form or other.[15] Amrit Bazar Patrika, a most popular nationalist newspaper of that time, accepted the drain theory as a cause of poverty of India and from 1870, it repeated it again and again. The drain theory was officially adopted by the Indian National Congress at its Calcutta session in 1896, when it proclaimed that the famine in India and the poverty of the people had been brought on by the drain of the wealth of the country which has been going on for years together.[16] D.E. Wacha, in his Presidential Address to the Indian National Congress, put the amount of the drain at Rs. 30 to 40 crores a year.[17]

It was Dadabhai, however, who popularized and continuously stressed on the drain theory. In 1905, Dadabhai declared that nearly 34 million sterling or Rs. 51.5 crores worth of Indian produce was being drained out of India annually.[18] He also hinted at the remedy. In the famous speech on the drain at the International Socialist Congress in 1904, he declared, "The remedy was to give India self-government. She should be treated like other British colonies. The Indians would maintain their connexion with England, but they resented being treated as slaves. They demanded the right to govern themselves, and to share in the general progress made by the nations of the earth.[19] After some time, in his message to the Calcutta session of the Indian National Congress. Dadabhai declared, "Without self-government the

Indians can never get rid of their present drain, and the consequent impoverishment, misery and destruction... The drain can only be stopped by the Government, by the people themselves...self-government is the only remedy for India's woes and wrongs.[20] Following Tilak's declaration of Swaraj, Dadabhai too demanded self-government in the Calcutta session of the Congress in 1906.

(C) Political Basis of Indian Nationalism

Nationalism, according to Tilak, was not a mere sentiment. It is a religion, "the dharma of the age", that comes from God. He interpreted that since nationalism represents readiness on the part of the individual to sacrifice his personal interest, his family, class and sectional interest to the larger interest of the nation,[21] it comes close to religion since religion also involves sacrifice and enlightenment. However, Tilak considered nationalism to be superior to religion. He wrote, "Love of nation is one's first duty. Next comes religions and governments." Tilak granted to this cult of nationalism a sacrament, signs and symbols.[22] Valentine Chirol remarks: "he added an intimate familiarity with the habits of thought and speech of his Mahrattas, and he knew how to play on their religious emotions when he gave a new meaning to the cult of their favourite god, the elephant-headed Ganesh, by making his festivals the occasion of popular demonstrations in which he grafted a new hatred of British rule on to the old hatred of Mohammadan domination. He used them especially to revive the memory of the great Shivaji, the glorious protector of the Brahman and of the sacred cow, who never laid his victorious sword aside until he had freed Maharashtra from the alien yoke."[23] The argument runs that Tilak reinforced Hindu customs and traditions. But to regard Tilak as an orthodox Hindu, on that account, may not be true.

Rajni Kothari points out that leaders in the Congress movement, chiefly Tilak and Gandhi, saw value in not rejecting the religious basis of nationalism and in drawing inspiration from tradition in nationalist action. Kothari appreciates the fact that there lay the need to bridge the enormous gap between traditional India and modern India which their approach bridged. Reinterpretation of tradition was a necessary task which Tilak's nationalism fulfilled. His powerful symbolism self-consciously connected the nationalist movement with India's great past.[24]

Tilak is also characterized as a cultural nationalist who infused Indian nationalism with the glow of a redefined and 'reformed' Hinduism and the assertion of a new-found 'Hindu identity'. Dumont sums up the position of Tilak in the following words:

> "We are led to understand how fundamentally the political actions of Tilak and Gandhi are based on an intellectual synthesis that was prepared in the nineteenth century and which is often called neo-Hinduism. Let us only characterize it schematically by saying that it is a synthesis in response to western challenge which is still more political and social than religious: an integration of the new social and political values within a reformed traditional and at least outwardly religious view; a reaffirmation of supposed Hindu values on a new level a victorious reaffirmation of traditional Hindu values was a preliminary condition of an active political struggle against foreign domination on the part of Hindus. One is led to speak of 'Hindu Nationalism', an expression which could well describe the common ground between tendencies as different as those of Tilak and Gandhi".[25]

Asghar Ali Engineer notes at several places that Tilak and Gandhi employed religio-cultural idiom to enthuse and mobilize Hindu masses as the Muslim.[26] Ulama employed the same idiom to enthuse and mobilize the Muslim. As against this, secular rational idiom was employed by Nehru. Engineer also adds that though secular idiom did find its followers, the mass of people were enthused by religio-cultural idioms only.

Research Questions

Tilak used Hindu symbols, and always was an ardent follower of the Gita ideal of Karma-Yoga and Vedas. He was criticized as a Hindu nationalist. We have to examine in this work whether it would be correct to regard Tilak as a 'Hindu nationalist', since the term connotes a derisive meaning and yokes Tilak's nationalism to Hinduism which robs it of universal character.

On the question of means also, controversy centres round Tilak's nationalism. Tilak had been criticised as a follower of violence. Tilak's ideal hero was the great Maratha King Shivaji. The murder of Afzal Khan by Shivaji was justified by Tilak, on the ground that Afzal Khan symbolized tyranny. But the use of this symbol is treated by Tilak's critics as a defence of violence. This thesis would attempt to answer the charge if Tilak was a promoter of violent means to gain even a noble cause.

The values and the ideas have rapidly changed in independent India. India proclaimed its goal of secularism, but the vices of Hindutva and charges of appeasement of minorities in the name of secularism have been raised. People are divided on the basis of language, caste and class. In this work, we shall examine how far Tilak's ideas are for or against the present tendencies. How much Tilak is useful or relevant in the recent controversies of the time is a burden of our inquiry in this research work.

After independence, socialism and secularism have become essential factors of Indian nationalism, but why were they not important in the minds of leaders like Tilak. And can we derive inspiration from Tilak and find correctives if certain distortions have erupted.

Tilak was against fraud and force in diplomacy, but if the opponent was taking recourse to them, he would not forbid their use in return. On that basis, Tilak's political thought came to be characterised as that of Democratic Realism. A point of inquiry in this research work is if it would be a right approach to judge Tilak and if there is similarity between political realism of Tilak and the pragmatic politics being practised today.

Footnotes

1. A.R. Desai, *Social Background of Indian Nationalism*, Bombay, Popular Book Depit, p. 260.
2. *Ibid.*, p. 261.
3. *Ibid.*, p. 260.
4. *Ibid.*, p.xxii-xxiii
5. *Ibid.*, p. 383.
6. *Ibid.*, p. 384.
7. Partha Chatterjee, *Nationalist Thought and Colonial World, A Derivated Discourse*, Delhi, Oxford University Press, p. 24.
8. *Ibid.*, p. 24.
9. *Ibid.*, p. 25.
10. *Ibid.*, p. 25.
11. *Ibid.*, p. 24.
12. Sudhir Chandra, *Dependence and Disillusionment*, Delhi, Manas Publications, p. 116.
13. Bipin Chandra, *The Rise and Growth of Economic Nationalism in India*, Delhi, Peoples Publishing House, p. 637.
14. *Ibid.*, p. 636.
15. *Ibid.*, p. 640.
16. *Ibid.*, p. 643.
17. *Ibid.*, p. 648.
18. *Ibid.*, p. 648.
19. *Ibid.*, p. 696.
20. *Ibid.*, p. 697.
21. S. N. Dubey, *Modern Indian Political Thinkers*, Delhi, Books' N Books, p. 67.
22. Ibid., p. 72.
23. Valentine Chirol, *India*, London, Ernest Benn, 1926, pp. 99-100.
24. Rajni Kothari, *Politics India*, Delhi, Orient Longman, 1970, p. 44.
25. L. Dumont, *Homo-Hierarchicus*, Oxford University Press, pp. 324-325.
26. Ramakant and B.C. Uproti (eds.), *Nation-Building in South Asia*, New Delhi, South Asian Publisher, 1990, p. 65.

2 Philosophical Bases of Tilak's Nationalism

Tilak's theory of nationalism was based on a strong philosophical foundation. He provided philosophical content to nationalism by combining the attainment of 'Swaraj' with the great ideals of Hindu religion.

Tilak's nationalism has a revivalistic orientation.[1] He wanted to bring to the front the message of the Vedas and Gita for providing spiritual energy and moral enthusiasm to the nation. Tilak was a Vedantist in his metaphysical views. His belief in human fellowship also followed from his Vedantism. He pleaded for the reconciliation between the ideal of nationalism and the Vedantic conception of human unity. In a speech, he once declared: "If the Vedantic ideal is higher, it necessarily includes the national ideal which is lower. The two are not irreconcilable if you know how to reconcile them. The two are not opposed to each other. One includes the other much in the same way as thousand includes five hundred. The two ideals are mutually consistent and both of them demand a kind of self-sacrifice and self-control. Both of them demand, in addition to self-control and self-sacrifice, a kind of higher altruistic feeling by which man is impelled to ignore selfish considerations and to work for persons and for objects which do not in the least savour of any egotistic aim. The feeling is one of love for humanity, for the equality of man before God, and it is the spirit of that feeling that governs the two ideals, Vedantic and national.[2]

Tilak linked the question of nationalism with the question of philosophical and spiritual values. He found the answer of the problem of attainment of Swaraj in the 'Gita' ideal of 'Karma-Yaga'. His ideas on non-violence were also guided by the principles of 'Gita' and other religious books. In this light, we have to examine the philosophical foundations of Tilak's idea of nationalism.

Non-Violence

Tilak expounded his ideas on non-violence clearly and sharply in his famous book 'Gita Rahasya'. He wrote: 'Harmlessness (Ahinsa) is the highest religion' is a principle which has been accepted as pre-eminent not only in our Vedic religion but in all other religions. The religious commandments given in the Buddhistic and Christian sacred books have given the first place to the commandment 'Thous shalt not kill' as has been done by Manu. Hinsa does not mean only destroying life but also includes harming the minds or the bodies of others. Therefore 'ahinsa' means not harming in any way any living being.'[3]

Tilak accepted that non-violence was the highest religion according to all the people in the world. "But", he says, "assuming for the sake of argument that some villain has come, with a weapon in his hand to kill you, or to commit rape on your wife or daughter, or to set fire to your house or to steal all your wealth, or to deprive you of your immovable property, and there is nobody who can protect you, then should you close your eyes and treat with unconcern such a villain saying: "ahinsa paramo dharmah" or should you, as much as possible, punish him if he does not listen to reason?" He quoted Manu who says, "Such an atatayin, that is villain, should be killed without the slightest compunction and without considering whether he is a preceptor (guru), or an old man or a child or learned Brahmin." According to him, the shastras enjoin that the killer does not incure the sin of killing, but the villain is killed by his own unrighteousness. He said that not only Manu but also modern criminal law has accepted the right of self-defence with some limitation. On these occasions, self-protection is considered to be of higher importance than harmlessness.[4]

This is the reason why Tilak never discouraged the revolutionaries, though, he, personally, always favoured non-violence. He thought that the revolutionaries weer working for a kind of self-protection. A protection from an alien rule, and his was not against the 'dharma' and so, he never hated them. Tilak cannot be said to be a propagator of violence but he could allow it if it was necessary at any one time.

On the point of violence, we find similarity between Tilak and the Bangalee nationalist, Bankim Chandra. He also said: "Ahinsa does not enjoin one to abhor violence at all times and in all circumstances." He had given an example that "When a tiger prepares to spring upon me, I must pull the trigger as quickly as possible, because if I do not destroy it, it will destroy me." Therefore, he told that "To use violence, to prevent one who does violence is not immoral, on the contrary, it is the highest moral duty."[5]

Although the place of absolute non-violence in politics is a matter of thinking, Gandhi was an advocate of absolute non-violence. He always preached non-violence in its absolute form but is it fulfilled when in the first world war he recruited soldiers for the British?[6]

As mentioned by Azad in his autobiography, the resolution of the Indian National Congress Working Committee passed on July 14, 1942, which must have had Gandhi's approval, implied that if the British government arrested the Congress leaders, people were free to adopt any method violent or non-violent. The Kashmir operation in 1947 was approved by Gandhi. He also repeatedly said that while it was best to resist evil non-violently, it was better to fight than to give in from cowardice or apathy.[7]

Addressing the Institute of Pacific Relations at Lucknow on October 3, 1950, Nehru admitted that while Gandhi preached non-violence and they followed him 'to some extent', they did not understand him'. "We see around us", he continued, "a world full of violence." On July 26, 1955 in the Lok Sabha, he said that the government of India was not pledged to non-violence and no government could be.[8]

Freedom

Tilak awakened the nation to its destiny and India's destiny was 'Swaraj'. It is true that Tilak always said that Swaraj did not imply the negation of ultimate British soverignty but people knew that Tilak wanted complete independence for India by his heart and soul. Tilak was a practical leader, therefore, he knew that it was invain to demand complete independence at that time. This is why Tilak always said: "Swaraj is the foundation and not the height of our future prosperity." He more clearly stated the meaning of Swaraj when he wrote: "Liberty is an adjunct of the soul. Where there is liberty, there is soul. It is an eternal doctrine and it is not afraid of anyone. Political philosophy must end in this very doctrine."[9]

Therefore, it is clear that he was a lover of freedom and wanted complete independence for India. He said in Nasik: "The body might grow old, descrepit and it might perish, but the soul is immortal. Similarly if there might be an apparent lull in our Home Rule activities, the freedom of the spirit behind it is eternal and indestructible, and it will secure liberty for us. Freedom is my birthright. So long as it is awake within me, I am not old. No weapon can cut this spirit, no fire can burn it, no water can wet it, no wind can dry it. I say that no C.I.D. can burn it. This principle will not disappear even it seems to be killed. We ask for Home Rule and we must get it."[10]

Therefore, we see that Tilak wanted to teach the people the philosophical principle that the spirit of Freedom is immortal and it never ends. he said, "The body dies but the Atma is immune, immortal, similarly the spirit of liberty that animates our activities and guides our movements can never grow old. The spirit of liberty is ever fresh and young and those that have drawn inspiration from it and have begun to work for its achievement through difficulties of every sort are bound to reap the fruit of their labour. Those that earnestly strive for liberty must become free. If you admit the truth of this proposition you must admit that liberty is the birthright of every man. The privilege of being free does not need to be granted by somebody else. Every man who is born, comes into the world with this elementary right. This innermost craving of the heart to be free, this intense desire to get one's liberty, is the essence of human nature. And as long as the spirit of freedom rules my heart, I shall refuse to admit that I have grown old."[11]

He talks about the Gita ideal of Atma: "The Bhagwat Gita tells you that this imperishable Atma cannot be destroyed by weapons nor can be burned by fire", and then he said that "What is called Atma in the religious philosophy is known as liberty in the science of politics. Atma exists everywhere; it does not need to be reborn. Similarly the love of liberty exists in every heart and I am only awakening you to the consciousness of its existence. Some people forget that they have this Atma or love of liberty - the reason being their ignorance."[12]

Thus, for Tilak, Atma and liberty is the same thing. The first is related to the religious philosophy and the second to the science of politics. He said in his speach at Nasik: "The science which ends in Home Rule is the Science of Politics, and not the one which ends in slavery. The Science of Politics consists of two parts. The first is Divine and the second is Demonic. The slavery of a Nation comes into the latter part. There cannot be a moral justification for the Demonic part of the Science of Politics. A Nation which might justify this is guilty of sin in the sight of God. Some people have the courage to declare what is harmful to them and some have not that courage. The political and religious teaching consists in giving the knowledge of this principle. All philosophies are included in the Science of Politics."[13]

Karma-Yoga

Tilak linked the question of Swaraj with 'Gita' ideal of Karma-Yoga. The science of Karma-Yoga is very important. This is a very comprehensive conception of Hindu philosophy.

The 'Gita' says:

कर्मन्येवाधिकारस्ते मा फलेषु कदाचन्।
मा कर्मफलहेतूर्भूर्मा ते संगोडस्त्वकर्मणि।।47।।

The four quartets of this stanza are mutually complementary; and therefore, without their overlapping each other, the entire import of Karma-Yoga is given in a short and beautiful form, nay, one may say that the four parts of this stanza are the catuh sutri of the Karma-Yoga.[14]

It is stated to begin with that 'your authority extends only to the performance of Action'; but the Blessed has pronounced in a clear way in the 2nd quartet of the stanza that 'your authority does not extend to the Fruit'; and then he has pronounced the 3rd proposition that 'do not be one who performs Action having in mind the Hope for Fruit'. But some one may advance the argument that because an Action and the fruit of it are interlinked, one must give up the Action, at the same time as giving up the Hope for Fruit. In order to make it clear that such an inference would not be correct, the clear advice has been given, that one should give up the Hope for Fruit but, at the same time, one should not insist on not doing Action, that is, on giving up Action.[15]

Therefore, the 'Gita' says in this stanza that one should perform his duty at any cost without having desire for Fruit. Tilak also, like the 'Gita', always used tc say: "Action alone must be our guiding principle, action disinterested and well-thought out."[16]

The proposition of Karma Yoga mentioned in the 49th stanza, namely, that 'The Reason is superior to the Action'.

दूरेण हयवरं कर्म बुद्धियोगाद्धनंजय।
बुद्धो शरणमन्विच्छ कृपणाः फलहेतवः।।49।।

It must be understood in this stanza as meaning, 'desire', or understanding. The goodness and badness of an act does not depend on the act itself, and though the act may be one and the same, it becomes good or bad according to the good or evil intention of the doer; therefore, the Reason is superior to the Action.[17]

Therefore, the 'Gita' says that any act becomes good or bad according to its intention, and this was the 'mahamantra' of Tilak. He always talked about the purification of intention. This was the purity of intention that Lord Krishna preached Arjuna to 'Fight'. It would be necessary to advance some cogent reason in support of this firm advice rather than placing before him the indecisive advice that it was just the same whether he fought or did not fight after he had acquired Realisation. Nay, the doctrine of the 'Gita' has come into existence only in order to explain why a wise man must perform a particular act, notwithstanding that he sees before his eyes the terrible consequences of it; and this is indeed the most important feature of the 'Gita'.[18]

This question of Arjuna is not something new. In the Yoga-Vasistha, Rama has asked the same question to Vasistha and in the Ganesgita, the king named Varenya has asked the same question to Ganesa and it appears from the works of Aristotle that this question has been raised in very ancient times in Europe in Greece, where philosophical ideas first originated. Yet in the book written by him subsequently on Politics, Aristotle himself says, "And it is equally a mistake to place inactivity above actions of the just and the wise are the realisation of much that is noble."[19]

August Comte, a well-known French philosopher of the last century, says in his book on Material Philosophy that "It is misleading to say that it is better to spend one's life in the contemplation of philosophy, and the philosopher, who adopts such a course of life, and abandons the doing of whatever public welfare it is possible for him to do, must be said to misuse the material which is at his disposal."[20]

It need not be said that the English philosophers Spencer, Mill and others aer of the same opinion as Comte. Nietzsche has gone beyond all these philosophers, and he has in his works so severely criticised those who are for giving up Action, that, accordig to him, it is not possible to refer to the supporters of Renunciation by any milder terms than 'fool of fools'.[21]

Therefore, Tilak justified his logic of Karma-Yoga, by giving the several examples of eastern as well as western philosophy. According to him: "Karma-Yoga has been our sacred heritage from time immemorial when we Indians were seated on the high pedestal of wealth and lore. Karma-Yoga or to put it in another way, the Law of Duty is the combination of all that is best in spiritual science, in actual action and in an unselfish meditative life. Compliance with this universal law leads to the realization of the most cherished ideals of Man. Swaraj is the natural consequence of diligent performance of duty. The Karma-Yogin strives for Swaraj, and the Sanyasin or spiritualist yearns for it."[22]

He, then defines Swaraj: "What is then this Swaraj? It is a life centred in Self and dependent upon Self." Then he gave the materialistic view of Swaraj, "There is Swaraj in this world as well as in the world hereafter. The Rishis who laid down the Law of Duty betook themselves to forests, because the people were already enjoying Swaraj or People's Domination, which was administrated and defended in the first instance by the Kshatria kings. Swaraj in the life to come cannot be the reward of a people who have not enjoyed it in this world. Such was the doctrine taught by our forefathers who never intended that the goal of life should be meditation alone."[23]

Tilak was a man of action. Therefore, he wanted the people also to be active. He said: "God does not help the indolent. You must be doing all that you can to lift yourself up, and then only you may rely on the Almighty to help you."[24] Tilak, however, knew that Swaraj might not come in one generation, but he did not care for it, because, he was a Karma-Yogi and the 'Gita' says, not to care for Fruits.

Therefore, he said : "You should not, however, presume that you have to toil that you yourself might reap the fruit of your labours. That cannot always be the case. Let us then try our utmost and leave the generations to come to enjoy that fruit. Remember, it is not you who had planted the mango-trees the fruit where of you have tasted. Let the advantage now go to our children and their descendants. It is only given to us to toil and work. And so, there ought to be no relaxation on our efforts, lest we incur the curse of those that come after us."[25] Therefore, action was necessary. One should perform his duty and care not for the result, because it may be possible that the fruit of his labour goes to the share of the next or other generation. So, one should only care for his action, and "This is called the immutable Dharma, and Karma-Yoga is nothing but the method which leads to the attainment of Dharma or material and spiritual glory,"[26] Tilak said. He wrote that "God has declared his will. He willed that self can be exalted only through its own efforts. Everything lies in your hands. Karma-Yoga does not look upon this world as nothing; it requires only that your motives should be untainted by selfish interest and passion. This is the true view of practical vedanta the key to which is apt to be lost in sophistry."[27]

Essence of Karma Yoga

That science by means of which we can decide such questions as: Which is the best and purest of the several 'yogas', means, or processes by which a particular Action can be performed; whether it can be always follwed; if not, what are the exceptions to it, and how they arise; why is that path which we call good, really good, or that which we call bad, really bad, and on the strength of what, is this goodness or badness to be decided and who is to do so or what is the underlying principles in it etc., is known as the 'Karma-Yoga-Shastra'.[28]

Good or bad are words in ordinary use and the following other words: propitious and unpropitious, or beneficial and harmful, or meritorious and non-meritorious or sin and virtue, or righteous and unrighteous, are used in the same sense. The same is the meaning conveyed by the word-couples doable and not doable (karya and akarya), duty and non-duty (kartavya and akartavya), just and unjust (nyayya and anyayya).[29]

Nevertheless as the variousd persons who have used these words have different ideas about the formation of the universe, there have also come into existence different ways in which the 'Karma-Yoga' science has been expounded. Whatever science is taken, the subject-matter of it can be discussed ordinarily in three ways:

1. Considering the various objects inthe physical world from the point of view that they really are as they are perceived by our organs, and that there is nothing beyond, is the first of these methods, which is known as "Adhi-Bhautika" (Positive or materialistic) way of considering them. For instance, when you look upon the Sun not as a deity, but as a round-mass of gross matter made up of the five primordial elements, and examine its various properties such as its heat, or light, or weight, or distance, or power of attraction, etc., that becomes the positive or material examination of the Sun. Take the tree as another illustration. It we do not consider the internal force in the tree which is responsible for its getting leaves etc., but consider the tree purely externally, that is, consider only the facts that whenthe seed is put into the earth, it takes root and becomes a sprout, which grows later on and goes through the visible changes of leaves, flowers, fruits etc., that is a purely material examination of the tree. The examination of the subject-matter in Chemistry of Physics or the Science of Electricity or other modern Science is of this kind. Nay, materialists imagine that when they have examined in this way the visible properties of any object, that is all they need to do and that is useless to further examine the objects in the world.[30]

2. When we discard this point of view, and examine what there is at the root of the object in the material world and whether the activities of these objects ae due to some inherent properties in them or there is some other power or principle behind those activities, then one has to transcend the material examination of the object. For instance, if we believe that in the gross or lifeless globe of the Sun made up of the five primordial elements, there exists a deity called the 'Sun' which dwells within it, and that this deity carries on the activities of the material Sun, such examination is called an AdhiDaivika (theological) examination of the object. According to this point of view, there are in the tree, water, air etc., innumerable deities, which are distinct from those objects, and which activate those objects.[31]
3. But, when instead of believing in this way that there are millions and millions of independent deities in all the various objects in the gross world, we believe that there exists in this world some Spiritual Force, i.e., factor of consciousness imperceptible to the organs, which carries on all the activities of the external world, and that this Spiritual Force exists in the human body in the shape of an Atman and acquaints the human being with the entire creation, and that this cosmos is kept going by that force, such consideration of the object is called an Adhyatmika (metaphysical) examination of the object. For instance, metaphysicians believe that the movements of the Sun and the Moon or even of the leaves of the tree are inspired by this unimaginable power and that there are not different and independent deities in the Sun or in other objects.[32]

These three ways of examining any subject-matter have been in existence from time immemorial and they seem to have been followed even in the Upanisads. For instance, in the Bhadaranyaka and other Upanisads while considering whether the organs of perception (Jnanendriya) or the vital force (prana) is superior, their respective strengths are considered, once from the point of view that they have deities like Agni etc. and again by considering their subtle forms and the consideration of the form of the Iswara at the end of the seventh chapter and in the beginning of the eighth chapter of the Gita is also from this point of view.[33]

Out of these three methods, our religious writers attach a higher importance to the metaphysical (adhyatmika) method of consideration than to others, relying on the authority "Adhyatma-Vidya-Vidyanam". But in modern times, the meaning of these three methods has to a certain extent changed and the well-known French Materialist Comte has given the highest importance to the positive exposition. He says that there is no sense in trying to find out the fundamental element, if any, which exists at the root of the world; and in as much as this element is always unknowable (agamya), it is neither possible nor proper to found on it the edifice of a science. When the aboriginal man for the first time saw trees, clouds, volcanoes, and other moving objects, he credulously began to believe that they were all deities. According to Comte,. this was the theological consideration of the universe. But man very soon gave up this idea and began to think that there must be some element in the shape of an Atman in all these objects. According to Comte, this is the second stage of the progress of human knowledge, and this stage is called by him the metaphysical stage. But when even after considering the universe in this way, actual practical scientific knowledge did not grow, man ultimately began to examine deeper and deeper only the visible properties of the objects in his world; and on that account man has now begun to exercise greater control over the external world, as a result of his having been able to invent steam-engines, telegraphs etc. Comte calls this the positive consideration and he has come to the conclusion that this method of consideration of any science or object is the most profitable one. According to Comte, we must adopt this method for scientifically considering Sociology or the science of Karma-Yoga; and after a careful consideration of the history of the world, this philosopher has drawn the following conclusion regarding the science of worldly life, from that point of view, namely, that the highest religion of every human being is to love the whole human race and to continually strive for the benefit of everybody. Mill, Spencer and other English philosophers may be said to support this opinion. On the other hand, Kent, Hegel, Schaupenhauer and other German philosophers have proved that this positive method of considering Ethics is inefficient and they have recently revived in Europe the method of basing Ethics or Metaphysics adopted by our Vedanta philosophers.[34] Therefore, we see that Tilak has given a long and comparative definition of 'Karma-Yoga' in his book 'Gita-Rahasya', and his idea of Swaraj was based on this particular philosophy of Karma-Yoga.

Dharma

Tilak mentioned 'Swaraj' not only as a right but as 'dharma' but when he said 'dharma', it did not connote the ordinary meaning of religion. The word 'Dharma' is in ordinary practice very often used to imply only the path leading to next-world happiness. When we ask someone, "What is your dharma (religion)?" Our intention is to ask him by what path he goes whether Vedic, Buddhist, Jain, Christian, Mahommedan or Parsi - for acquiring happiness in the next world; and the reply which he gives is also from the same point of view, but the word 'dharma' is not to be understood in such a restricted sense, and it is very often used for indicting the morality as in the phrases 'rajadharma', 'prajadharma', 'desadharma', 'jnatidharma', 'kuladharma', 'mitradharma', etc. If these two meanings of the world 'dharma' are to be individually explained, the dharma relating to the life after death may be called 'moksadharma' or simply 'modsa', and the dharma relating to this worldly life.[35]

Tilak said that Ethics may be given the name of 'dharma' simply. For instance, in enumerating the four ideals of manhood (purusartha), we say 'dharma', 'artha', 'kaam', 'moksa'. If moksa is meant to be included in the first word 'dharma', then it would not be necessary to mention 'moksa' as an independent ideal at the end. Therefore, we must say that the writers of our scriptures use the word 'dharma' here as meaning the numerous ethical duties which form part of our worldly life. The same meaning is conveyed by the words 'kartavya-karma' (duty), niti (ethics), 'nitidharma' (morality) or 'sadkarma' (good conduct) used nowadays.[36]

The word 'dharma' has appeared on numerous occasions in the Mahabharata, and whenever it has been said there that a particular person is found to do a particular thing according to his 'dharma', the word 'dharma' means ethical science (kartavya-sastra) or the then sociology (samaj-vyavastha-sastra).[37] Therefore, we see that according to Tilak, when a man performs his duty rightly, then it could be said that he fulfilled his 'dharma'. So also in the Manu-Smrti and other Smrti texts, in mentioning the specific duties of four castes, Brahmin, Ksatriya, Vaisya and Sudra, the word 'dharma' has been used on many occasions and in many places; and even in the Bhagavadgita the word 'dharma' has been used as meaning 'the duties of the four castes in this world', where the Blessed Lord is telling Arjuna to fight, having regard to what his 'dharma' is.[38] Tilak said, "In short, when we use the word 'dharma' from the worldly point of view, we consider in what way society will be maintained and benefited."[39]

Sri Krishna also says in the Karnaparva, "The word Dharma comes from the root dhri, to hold or uphold, and all human beings are held together by dharma. That by which the holding together takes place is dharma." Therefore when this dharma cesses to be observed, the binding ropes of society may be said to have become loose, and when these binding ropes are loosened, society will be in the same position as the planetary system consisting of the Sun and the planets would be in the sky without the binding force of gravitation or as a ship would be on the ocean without a rudder. Therefore, Vyasa in the Bharata gives the advice that in order that society should not come to an end by reaching such a lamentable state, artha, if it has to be acquired, must be acquired by 'dharma', that is without disturbing the arrangement of society and if the desires have to be satisfied, that should also be done consistently with 'dharma'.[40] Tilak thus wrote, "We apply the common word 'Dharma' chiefly to worldly morality or to system laid down for the maintenance of society. Not only in the Sanskrit treatises Mahabharata and Bhagwadgita, but also in vernacular works is the word 'dharma' always used as meaning worldly duties or laws."[41]

It has become usual, whether in Sanskrit or in Prakrit literature, to use the word 'dharma' as indicting the rules of morality which have been laid down by high and reverend persons, with reference to various matters, for the maintenance of society. These rules, which have been laid down by reverend people and which have become acceptable on all hands and are known as 'respectable behaviour' (sistacara), are, from this point of view, the root of dharma; and therefore, in the Mahabharata and also in the Smriti treatises there are such statements as: "morality springs from custom" or "rules of custom are the highest morality" or "the Vedas, the Smritis, good conduct and that which we ourselves desire."[42]

We must also here consider another definition of the word 'dharma' which is come across in ancient treatises. This is the definition given by Mimansa school. That school says: "Condanalaksonartho dharmah". 'Codana' means 'inspiring', that is, some authoritative person saying or ordering: "Do this" or "Do not do this". So long as no one had laid down such a limitation or such a limitation has not come into existence, one is at liberty to do what he likes. This means that dharma originally came into existence as a result of such limitations and this definition of morality is to a certain extent similar to the opinions of the well-known English writer Hobbs. The human being in the aboriginal condition behaved according to the particular frame of mind rulling at the time. But when he later on found out that such unrestricted behaviour was not beneficial on the whole, he came to the definite conclusion that it was in the best interests of everybody to lay down and observe certain restrictions on the self-inspired actions of the organs, and every human being began to observe these limitations which have gained ground on account of general acceptance (sistacara), or for some other reason, as if they were laws; and when such limitations grew in number, they formed themselves into a code.[43] For example, the institution of marriage was not at first in vogue, but was brought into existence by Svetaketu, and also that the prohibition against drink was first laid down by Sukracarya.

Thus, we find that Tilak's 'dharma' is not limited only to the religious scriptur and worshipping the God, but he explained it in a broad sense. When he used the word 'dharma', it did not mean the religion, but it indicated the human duty, morality and right action. This is why, he also used to mention that 'Swaraj' is not only our right, but 'dharma', because he thought that it is the duty of every Indian to make effort for attainment of 'Swaraj', and thus, 'Swaraj' ultimately became the dharma of the people of India.

Interpreting the Vedas

For obtaining an insight into the political ideologies, techniques of leadership and general political personality of Tilak, it is essential to have in mind some fundamental notions enunciated by him in his research works on the Vedas. He drew intellectual sustenance and spiritual fervour from these works, which enabled him to survive the political ordeals of his life. Furthermore, through these researches, he directly and indirectly sought to strengthen the cultural and spiritual basis of Indian nationalism. Hence, we propose to present here a short review of his ideas regarding the Vedic antiquities.

Tilak's 'Orion' was published in 1893. In the 'Orion' it was shown that astronomical statements pointed out that the vernal equinox was in constellation of Orion (about 4500 B.C.) during the period of the Vedic hymns and it had receded to the constellation of the Pleiades in the days of the works entitled Brahmanas. But it was also essential to trace the genesis of Aryan civilization beyond 4500 B.C.[44] Tilak did this work in his famous book, 'The Arctic Home in the Vedas', which was published in 1903.

On the basis of the researches in Geology and Archaeology, he arrived at the hypothesis that the ancestors of the Aryans lived in an Arctic home in the inter-glacial period. His conviction was confirmed by the evidences of the Avesta. The main geological historical point sought to be established in 'The Arctic Home' is that the period of primitive Aryan life goes much further beyond 4500 B.C. This view is substantiated on the basis of the theory of an American geologist that the commencement of the Post-Glacial period cannot be placed at a date earlier than 8000 B.C. On the basis of American geological researches about the glacial and postglacial epoch, Tilak arrives at the hypothesis that the primitive Aryan home was both Arctic and inter-glacial. Dr. Warren, of the Boston University, in his book 'Paradise Found or the Cradle of the Human Race in North Pole' anticipated Tilak to some extent. On purely mythological grounds, Prof. Rhys in his 'Hibbert Lectures on Celtic Heathendom' suggests some spot within the Arctic circle as the primitive Aryan home. Th. Poesche, L Geigev, J.G. Cuno, A.V. Gutschmied and Penka have also challenged the theory of the Asiatic home of the Aryans.[45]

In 'The Arctic Home of the Vedas' Tilak had stated that from 8000 B.C. to 5000 B.C. is the period of the migration of the Aryan peoples from Arctic regions to the various countries in Europe and Asia. It proves that Aryan civilization is an ancient civilization, about whom, it is said that they are the most ancient civilization in the world. The begining of the Egyptian and Babylonian civilization is traced to the period roundabout 4000 B.C. This anticipation of Tilak strengthens the basis of Hindu culture directly and by and by ultimately the basis of Hindu nationalism. This theory of Tilak proves that Hindu culture is, perhaps, the most ancient culture of the world.

Tilak had given the strong and scientific evidence in support of his Arctic theory:

> "We started with the tradition about the night, the night of the gods, or a day and a night of six months each and found it could be traced back to the Indo-Iranian, if not to the Indo-Germanic, period. A close examination of the dawnhymns in the Rigveda next disclosed the fact that the Usha, or the deity presiding over the dawn is often addressed in the plural number in the Vedic hymns, and that this could be accounted for only on the supposition that the Vedic dawns were a closely connected band of many dawns - a supposition, which was found to be fully borne out by express passages in the Vedic literature, stating, in unambiguous terms, that the Vedic dawns were 30 in number, and that in ancient times a period of several days elapsed between the first appearance of light on the horizon and the rising of the sun. We have also found that the dawn is expressly described in the Rigveda as moving round like a wheel, a characteristic, which is true only in the case of the Polar dawn. These facts sufficiently prove the acquaintance of the Vedic bards with the physical phenomena, witnessable only in the Arctic regions. But to make the matter more certain, I have quoted and discussed Vedic passages, which go to prove that the long Arctic nights and the corresponding long days of varying duration, as well as a year of ten months or five seasons were equally known to the poets of the Rigveda. An examination of the ancient sacrificial system and especially of the annual Sattras and night-sacrifices further showed that in old times

yearly sacrificial dessions did not last for twelve months, as at present, but were completed in nine or ten months; and the hundred night-sacrifices were, at that time, really performed, as their name indicates, during the darkness of the long night. The legends of Dirghatamas and Aditi's sons and the tradition about the sacrificial sessions of the Navagvas and the Dashagvas also pointed to the same conclusion. We have seen that the half-year long day and night, the long dawn with its revolving splendours, the long continuous night matched by the corresponding long day and associated with a succession of ordinary days and nights of varying lengths and the total annual period of sunshine of less than twelve months are the principal peculiar characteristics of the Polar or the Circum-Polar calendar: and when express passages are found in the Vedas, the oldest record of early Aryan thoughts and sentiments, showing that each and every one of these characteristics was known to the Vedic bards, who themselves lived in a region where the year was made up of three hundred and sixty or three hundred and sixty-five days, one is irresistibly led to the conclusion that the poets of the Rig-Veda must have known these facts by tradition and that their ancestors must have lived in regions where such phenomena were possible."[46]

Thus, we find that Tilak proved the Arctic Home of Aryans by giving some strong evidence. He also admitted that "It is not to be expected that the evidence on each and every one of these points will be equally conclusive, especially as we are dealing with facts which existed thousands of years ago,"[47] but he said: "I trust that if my interpretations are examined without any bias and in the light of the latest scientific researches, they will be found to be far more natural and simple than those in vogue at present. It did not start with any preconceived notion in favour of the Arctic theory, nay I regarded it as highly improbable at first; but the accumulating evidence in its support eventually forced me to accept it."[48]

Tilak proves that the Aryan civilization is the most ancient civilization in the world. If the Aryan civilization is the most ancient civilization then the fact remains that Hindu culture is an oldest culture, because the Hindus believe that the Aryans are their forefathers, and it proves that the Indian culture is older than any other European culture. Here become false all the claims of British people to be a superior and cultured race than Indians. Thus, we see that this Vedic research of Tilak gave more strength to the basis of Indian nationalism.

Was Tilak a Hindu Nationalist?

Tilak had a deep faith in Hindu religion. He based his nationalistic thoughts on the ideal of Gita and Vedas. He had intense pride in Hindu religion and culture and because he was a Hindu Brahmin by religion, so, his opponent dressed him in a garb of Hindu nationalist. But it is a matter of discussion that if one has deep faith in any religion or if one believes in one religion, is it enough to declare the person to be a communalist, as people like Palm Dutt, V. Chirol and Powel Price had declared?

Powel Price says that "The Muslim League was an answer to the Indian National Congress, necessary because the possibility of self-government raised the spirit of seperation which the intolerance of Tilak had emphasized." Zacharia says that Tilak was the spokesman of an anti-Moslem retaliation. Chirol aiso tried to picturise Tilak as a communal nationalist.[49] According to Palm Dutt, Tilak and Aurobindo were responsible to cut off the Moslem masses from the dominant stream of the national movement. But all these interpretations are not looking pure and correct, because of the statements of the Muslim leaders of that time.

Jinnah, M.A. Ansari and Hasan Imam have eloquently testified to the nationalistic sentiments and spirit of compromise of the Lokamanya, because due to his wise counsel and moderation the Lucknow Pact could be agreed upon. Shaukat Ali and Hasrat Mohani regarded Tilak as their political guru.

Saukat Ali says: "I would like to mention again for the hundredth time that both Mohammed Ali and myself belonged and still belong to Lokamanya Tilak's political party." Hasrat Mohani says: "I, even at that early age, chose the Lokamanya as the ideal leader for me... During that period I had ample opportunities of appreciating the thought and ability of almost all Indian political leaders and basing my remarks on that close personal study, I can state without the least fear of contradiction, that I found the Lokamanya greater and superior to every other leader in ever respect... When I declare that all through Tilak's life I was both intellectually and practically a blind follower of his, anyone can well judge thereby, of that love that I cherished towards him." Hasrat Imam says, "Let me say, and it is with great pride, that Lokamanya Tilak is my father in point of politics."[50]

It is a notable factor that if Tilak was anti-Muslim, he could never have commanded the confidence of the great Muslim leaders of that time. Besides this we all know that Tilak had proposed the Congress resolution for the release of the Ali brothers. He also was eager to support the Khilafat movement too. Abul Kalam Azad says: "Apart from Ghandiji, Lokamanya Tilak and other Congress leaders also supported the stand of Indian Muslims on the question of the Khilafat."[51]

The above discussion points to the fact that the charge of being a hindu nationalist on Tilak was not true. It is true that he had a deep faith in and regard for Hinduism, but it does not means that he was an anti-Muslim or against the other religions. Even in the present days, when secularism is included in the preamble of our Constitution, nobody can say that secularism meant to be anti-religious or a secular man has to be against the religion. The meaning of secularism is that one should have respect for all the religions and doesn't try to harm those people who are not belonging to his religion. As our Prime Minister Narasimha Rao said on the occasion of the Independence Day, in his speech, from the historical Red Fort, that "Secularism does not mean irreligiousness."

So, how can be brand Tilak as a mere Hindu nationalist? No one could be able to give the evidence, when the people of Muslim or any other community were harmed by Tilak. Tilak never showed any disrespect towards other religions in his speeches or writings. Then how he became a Hindu nationalist? Was it only because he was a Hindu by religion? Mrs. Annie Besant had also a deep respect and love for Hindu religion and she also used to cite the examples of Hindu religious books and epics, but no one tried to call her a Hindu nationalist or an anti-Muslim. Thus, we can say that Tilak was an Indian nationalist and not merely a Hindu nationalist.

P.J. Jagirdar distinguished Tilak's nationalism between political nationalism and cutlural nationalism. Political nationalism was generated by the political situation and had political aspirations, while cultural nationalism was the love for country and pride of cultural heritage and the confidence that traditional culture had the power to guide the present. Tilak's political nationalism was what we may call composite nationalism inclusive of men of all faiths; while his cultural nationalism was Hindu nationalism.[52] There is a clear evidence of Tilak's composite political nationalism. He says, in 1892, "We call ourselves brothers of one nation, because we are subjects of the same king... Under the sovereign regime of her Majesty the Queen, peace has been established throughout India and Hindus, Musalmans, Parsis, Sikhs and men of all castes and Professions are by our rulers thrown into one class, so that their interests are intertwined... Whatever men of all castes and faiths want to do, they must do it with one herat... We are brought together by the British rule; the binding tie of that rule is necessary to remove our feeling of separateness; and under the present circumstances if we are to make any efforts to remove our backward condition, we can do it only while this bondage is maintained." Tilak maintained this position till the end, as is shown by his role in making the Lucknow Pact.[53]

While his political nationalism was the outcome of political awareness, his cultural nationalism came from his heart. His deep attachement and devotion to ancient Hindu culture was developed in the environment of childhood. His father's and Vishnushastri Chiplunkar's influence further strengthened this attachment, and Hindu culture became a matter of prestige. He felt indignant at the invasion of western culture and determined to fight it. Any criticism of Hindu culture and civilization drove him to fury. He appreciated the new, evern though western, critical methods of studying history and society, but at heart he was an admirer of the Hindu tradition.[54]

In one way this cultural nationalism, though separate, is connected with his political nationalism. In politics his aim was not only "to make efforts to remove our backward conditions" as quoted earlier; the ultimate and the then unrevealed aim was to overthrow the foreign rule. It is true that common subjection to foreign, and therefore, exploiting rule may create the necessary revolt in which subjects of all faiths and provinces will take part. But appeal to ancient culture, especially to ancient religion, is a very strong force. Religious fervour when added to political farvour would work wonderes.[55] But Tilak's cultural nationalism was unconnected with his political nationalism in any other way. He did not aim at attaining national freedom without the help of Muslims. Secondly, he did not aim at establishing a Hindu raj. If he organised Hindus it was for the specific purpose of defence during riots, against the admittedly fanatic Muslim masses, and that too because the British officeials, for their own political motives, were partial towards the Muslims.[56]

Conclusion

Tilak's theory of nationalism was based on a strong philosophical foundation. He was a supporter of non-violence but was not against violence absolutely, in special conditions. He was a lover of liberty and claimed India's right to independence, not only for the material well-being of the people, but also for their spiritual and moral upliftment. He linked the philosophy of 'Swaraj' with the Gita ideal of 'Karma-Yoga' and 'Swaraj' was not only a right but dharma, according to Tilak. Tilak's dharma was not related only with religion but it was related with human duty. He strengthenes his philosophy of nationalism by giving the evidence of the Vedas. His Vedic researches strengthenes the basis of Indian nationalism and specially the Hindu nationalism. But we have argued that it is not correct to regard Tilak as a Hindu natioalist.

Footnotes

1. V.P. Varma, *The Life and Philosophy of Lokamanya Tolak*, Agra, Lakshmi Narain Agrawal Education Publication, 1978, p. 442.
2. *Ibid.*, p. 444.
3. B.G. Tilak, *Gita Rahasya*, Translated by Bhalchandra Sitaram Sukthanakar, Poona, Tilak Mandir, p. 42.43.
4. *Ibid.*, p. 43.
5. Chatterjee, *op. cit.*, p. 72.
6. K. Satchidananda Murthy, *Indian Foreign Policy*, Calcutta, Scientific Book Agency, p. 44.
7. *Ibid.*, p. 44.
8. *Ibid.*, p. 45.
9. Theodore L. Shay, *The Legacy of The Lokamanya*, Bombay, Oxford University Press, p. 187.
10. B.G. Tilak, *Writings and Speeches*, Madras, Ganesh and Company, p. 271-72.
11. D.V. Tahmankar, *Lokamanya Tilak*, London, John Murray, 1956, p. 235-36.
12. *Ibid.*, p. 236.
13. Tilak, Writings and Speeches, *op. cit.*, p. 276.
14. Tilak, Gita Rahasy, *op. cit.*, p. 895.
15. *Ibid.*, p. 895.
16. Tilak, Writings and Speeches, *op, cit.*, p. 278.
17. Tilak, Gita Rahasya, *op. cit.*, p. 897.

18. *Ibid.*, p. 417.
19. *Ibid.*, p. 418-19.
20. *Ibid.*, p. 419.
21. *Ibid.*, p. 420.
22. Tilak, Writings and Speeches, *op. cit.*, p. 276.
23. *Ibid.*, p. 277.
24. *Ibid.*,
25. *Ibid.*, p. 277-78.
26. *Ibid.*, p. 278.
27. *Ibid.*, p. 278-79.
28. Tilak, Gita Rahasya, *op. cit.*, p. 83
29. *Ibid.*
30. *Ibid.*, p. 84.
31. *Ibid.*, p. 84-85
32. *Ibid.*, p. 85.
33. *Ibid.*
34. *Ibid.*, p. 85-87
35. *Ibid.*, p. 88.
36. *Ibid.*, p. 88-89.
37. *Ibid.*, p. 89.
38. *Ibid.*,
39. *Ibid.*, p. 90
40. *Ibid.*, p. 90-91
41. *Ibid.*, p. 93
42. *Ibid.*, p. 94
43. *Ibid.*, p. 94-95
44. Varma, *op. cit.*, p. 464.
45. *Ibid.*,
46. B.G. Tilak, *The Arctic Home in the Vedas,* Poona, Messrs. Tilak Bros. p. 234.
47. *Ibid.*, p. 236.
48. *Ibid.*, p. 237.
49. Varma, *op. cit.*, p. 442.
50. *Ibid.*, p. 443-44.
51. Abul Kalam Azad, *India Wins Freedom,* Calcutta, Orient Longman, 1960, p. 8.
52. N.R. Inamdar (ed.), *Political Thought and Leadership of Lokamanya Tilak,* New Delhi, Concept Publishing Company, 1988, p. 243.
53. *Ibid.*, p. 243.
54. *Ibid.*, p. 244.
55. *Ibid.*
56. *Ibid.*

3 Social Bases of Tilak's Nationalism

India being an old society, it was natural that Indian nationalism should be based on a social basis. Right in the middle of the eighteenth century, nationalism in the form of social reform had emerged in India. Raja Ram Mohan Roy had started combating various social evils like sati, early marriage of girls, etc. Years later Tilak too clothed his nationalism with a social background. However, controversy exists around the social stands of Tilak. Tilak's critics condemned him as an orthodox. We can examine how far this charge is true in the light of his total social outlook.

The battle between social reform and orthodoxy was joined when Tilak grew to manhood. Many of the lively discussions between Tilak and Agarkar in their student days in the Deccan College were centred on it. Agarkar was an out and out champion of social reforms, but Tilak felt that political reform ought to receive prior attention. Tilak stood for the regeneration of Hindu society. But he deeply cherished its religious tenets, philosophical traditions and moral values and held that such changes as were necessary should come about gradually and with consent rather than compulsion. He believed that mass education was the best lever of social reforms and that in promoting it, an ounce of practice was worth a ton of precept. The gulf between principles and action of the champions of reforms invited his derision. Tilak was against the imposition of social reforms by the British rulers, not merely because they were alien and irresponsible but also because of their fundamentally different religious and social background.[2]

Charges of Orthodoxy Against Tilak

The first few years of Tilak's public life were occupied not so much by political struggle as by the controversy over social reform. Numerous provocations for this were forthcoming from the Rakhmabai-Dadaji case in 1886 to the Vedokta episode in 1901.

The Rakhmabai Case

The Rakhmabai case in which the issue was the husband's plea for the restitution of conjugal rights, created a great sensation. Rakhmabai's argument was that she was married to Dadaji without her consent and that, therefore, she should not be forced to live with him. This claim was clearly against Hindu Law and the High Court overruled the first judgment in her favour. But public sympathy was aroused in favour of Rakhmabai and even a fund was raised for her. In this case Tilak welcomed the High Court's verdict as upholding Hindu law and customs. In a bitter argument with Ranade, he drew on his deep knowledge of the scriptures to rebut the view that there should be no compulsion for an unwilling wife to stay with her husband.

Sharda Sadan Controversy

The controversy about female education centred round the activities of Pandita Ramabai, a woman of great personality and talent who had an unusual career. She founded her famous Sharda Sadan with the object of taking care of "destitute high caste widows". To avoid any misunderstanding about the aims and objects of the school, it was made clear at the start that the school would not actively preach Christianity or try to make converts. But the whole atmosphere of the institution was so charged with a typical missionary spirit that it was bound to make a deep impression on the inmates of the Sadan, some of whom of their own accord began to read the Bible and attend Church prayers.[4]

Her work was praised and admired by many but there were alos some who looked upon it with some degree of scepticism. Kesari (edited by Tilak) was among the doubters who suspected that the school might be used to benefit Christian converts, but had decided to say nothing against it until tangible evidence came to light. In December 1887, the Christian weekly of New York published a report on the progress of the Sadan in the course of which it said, "At present there are seven young widows in the Sharda Sadan, two of whom have expressed their love of Christianity. They regularly attend the daily prayers with Ramabai. The institution gives full freedom of faith and that this freedom of faith has done no harm to anybody suggests that the Sadan is clearly a Christian institute."[5]

Kesari drew attention to this report and a strong protest was voiced against the activities of Ramabai. Letters began to appeaer in the newspaper accusing her of being a hypocrite. Further support for the charge of hypocrisy against Pandita Ramabai was provided by one of her relatives, Krishnabai, who was an employee in the Sadan and looked after the institution's provisions and supplies. In a signed letter in Kesari, she said: "Hindu girls were not allowed to observe their religious rites and festivals in the Sadan. Nor were they allowed to visit Hindu temple." Tilak also published extracts from Ramabai's speeches which left no room for doubt that she had become and active missionary for spreading the Gospel and so, by converting Hindu women, was directly undermining Hindu society. When Tilak first attacked the Sharda Sadan, many so called social reformers accused him of being a reactionary, they called him the enemy of progress and the champion of orthodoxy, but soon realised not only that his exposure of the Sadan was well-founded, but that in making it he had done a service to Hindu society by his timely warning.[6]

The Age of Consent Bill

Heartened by his success in exposing Ramabai, which gave him greater confidence and authority, Tilak took up a bold stand in the controversy over the Age of Consent Bill, which was moved in the Imperial Legislative Council on January 9, 1891. The Bill received the enthusiastic support of many veteran reformers but was violently opposed by Tilak. He drew attention to the harmful effects of early marriage which ended in many cases in maternal and infantile mortality. The evil was so widespread that it affected the whole framework of society. He argued that "Education and not legislation is the proper method for eradicating the evil." His greatest objection to the Bill was that it gave officials of a foreign race the chance to interfere in the religious life and beliefs of the Hindu society. He also pointed out that as the Hindu population was in general not yet ready for the reforms the Bill should be made applicable only to those who believed in its necessity. His idea was that as education spread the people would gradually follow the example of the progressive sections of the community and the presence on the Statute Book of such a measure would help them to give up the old and harmful customs.[7]

All over Bombay presidency, Tilak set to work energetically to organise the orthodox Hindu opposition. Public meetings were held to condemn the Bill and were attended by thousands. There was nothing political in this opposition, but the very fact that the people were opposing a Bill put forward by a powerful Government, had a tremendous psychological effect in bringing new supporters to the campaign. Like a snowball, the agitation grew in size and momentum. It spread from Maharashtra to Bengal, Madras and other provinces in India. It touches the chords of unanticipated sections. In the Imperial Legislative Council, the European benches were shocked to see Romesh Chandra Mitra a man of moderate views and gentle manners siding with the opposition. He warned the members of the Government that he would oppose the Bill tooth and nail and that, if they still persisted in passing it into law, "it would create deep discontent among the people of India." Dramatically, he asked the Government to imagine what the British people would say and do if their customs and religious scruples were similarly flouted by an alien government, "if (he instanced) a law were enacted in Britain requiring dead bodies to be cremated rather than buried." But all these criticism and bitter opposition of people could not restrict the passing of the Bill and the Bill was passed on March 19, 1891.

In retrospect we can say that time has proved how right Tilak was. He was absolutely right in saying that it was not proper to rely on legislation alone for eradicating the evil. If after about hundred years of this legislation, child marriage still persists in the country, this is due to lack of education. Hence, Tilak emphasized that people must be educated to get rid of social evils. This goes to show that Tilak was a practical social reformer, and not an orthodox or a reactionary in social matters. It has been proved by the post-independence experience in India also that making a law or passing a Bill is not a solution of a social problem. For solving social problems, we have to change the mass opinion of the people. After passing of the Bill, Tilak realized that the Government and their reformist friends had won the battle but he was determined to deny them the fruits of victory. He therefore issued a ten-point programme and invited the reformers to subscribe to it. At a public meeting in Poona, he proposed a resolution recommending punishment for them who broke the new marriage law which had been enacted on the initiative of the reformers.[9] But those who were loudest in their support of the Age of Consent Bill were the first to refuse to put their signatures to this resolution. Tilak mentioned that the reforms were attacking only the fringe of the central problem rather than its core. He had no time for reforms by kind permission of the British Government. Indian problems must be solved by Indians. Therefore, for Tilak, the essential reform, and the one that must come first was the freedom of the country.

Supporter of Widow Remarriage

Tilak was not against widow-remarriage also. He is reported to have told his friends (of course in a lighter vein) that he would arrange for the remarriage of one thousand widows on the day India gained political independence.[10] In 1890, he said in a speech in Poona: "There has been much talk about social reform. But we have to bear in mind that we have to reform the masses and if we dissociate ourselves from them, reform would become impossible. The outstanding example of this is the fact that though widow-marriage is a desirable reform, most of the reformers do not practise it on their families. I, therefore, think that each one should begin reforms with himself, convert others through practice rather than by theory. Advocates of reform should live up to their own preaching."[11] He further said, "While the widow-remarriage movement was at its height, it was myself who proposed to the reformers to come to a compromise with the Shankaracharya on a reasonable basis. In my opinion, the evil of prohibition of widow-remarriage is not a general one bu tit is confined only to Brahmins and such other castes as have thought it fit to imitate Brahmin customs and manners. What I proposed, therefore, was that though widow-marriage is not sanctioned by the later Hindu law, yet a compromise could be adopted by including it in the forms of marriage sanctioned by the Shastras and thus removing, with the sanction of the orthodox, all disqualifications arising from social ostracism."[12]

Tilak was against untouchability and caste distinction. The main object of starting Ganapati festival in 1893 was to bring people of all the castes and creeds of Hindu society on one platform. An incident of 1894 illustrates Tilak's reformist stand. In 1894, the Ganapati procession was taking place, with thousands of young men and women singing devotional songs and playing music. Tilak was accompanying the procession when suddently his attention was attracted by a shrill cry from a window in one of the houses on the processional route. He looked up and saw a boy of seven or eight crying loudly while his mother tried to pacify him. Tilak stopped to ask why the boy was crying. The mother did not know what to say-she was shy and timid, perhaps terrified. At last she told him that her son wanted his Ganapati to be taken to the river for the immersion ceremony along with other Ganapatis but she dared not let him do this as her family belonged to the untouchable class. Tilak was moved to tears; he could not bear to see an innocent child suffer. He went into the house, took the Ganapati idol and placed it by the side of his own and the boy joined the procession holding on to Tilak's hand.[13]

Later, in 1918, addressing a special conference for untouchables in Bombay, he declared before an audience of more than seven thousand people: "If God were to tolerate untouchability I would not recognise him as God at all... Although I have appeared amongst you in person for the first time, believe me, you have been in my mind all the time..., I do not deny that it was the Brahman rule that introduced the practice of untouchability. This is a cancer in the body of Hindu society and we must eradicate it at all costs."[14]

Tilak was elected to the Legislative Council for the second time in 1897, but one who was not satisfied even on the Congress platform could not be expected to be happy with the work in the Council chamber. Very soon two great disasters in the form of a great famine followed by plague visited Maharashtra. In these twin disasters, when people ran helterskelter leaving the dead and the dying to their own fate, Tilak stood firm and by his personal courage, showed a noble example of selfless service.[15]

Fighting the Famine

Famines have always been a regular feature of Indian economy. from 1873 to 1878 there were famines of varying degrees of intensity in different provinces of India and this experience of famines had made Government formulate a Famine Code, after considering the question of famine relief on scientific lines. The difference between the famine of 1876 and that of 1896 according to Tilak was that the Government was now duty-bound to help the ryat under the terms of the Famine Relief Code. The Kesari, therefore, tried to give a summary of the Code for the benefit of its readers and also gave a prominent place to the complaints of the sufferers. It also tried to point out the shortcomings and mistakes of the Code. Government machinery was, as always, slow-moving and the bungling of officials frittered away whatever little relief the people were entitled to receive. The Kesari, Therefore, sounded timely notes of warning against the lower officials, habit of riding roughshod over the popular interests and urged the people to put up a determined stand against the high-handedness of the Government. Tilak tried his best to dissuade people from riots or looting the rich. The way he pointed out was to go to the Government and make applications to the collector urging him to give them remission in land revenue, to provide them with work and to grant them 'taqai loans'. The machinery of the newly created Sarvajanik Sabha was used effectively by him to ventilate the legitimate grievances of the people, to represent to the Government genuine cases of tax remission and suspension of land revenue in famine-stricken areas.[16] The workers of the Sabha, like the graduate Ramdasis of Tilak's idea, went to the villages and tried to explain to the people the famine code and also brought home to them that it was the duty of the Government to relieve their distress.

"Remember", wrote Tilak on the 15th December 1896, "that this Government is based on law and not aggression. If you have to fight you must also fight legally. Then alone we shall get our rights." He referred to the message sent by the queen and said that it was the desire of Her Majesty that no one should suffer in her kingdom. The bureaucracy, he reminded the people, would try to recover the land revenue from them by filing suits, or by threats or even by shooting them. "But let the people remember that if they should be determined to fight for their rights even at the risk of being shot at, it is the duty of leaders to help them fight. It is possible that even while fighting legally the tables may be turned against us but people must be ready for this. If they are not, then according to the English maxim, instead of bread they will get a stone. Charity of philanthropic people, however laudable, will do little. It is the Government that the people should look to."[17]

Even though Tilak was trying to keep strictly within the limits of the law, this language of his was fiery and it must have done much to make the people bold and defiant. Intellectual ideas and abstract principles of freedom, justice or equality have little or no appeal to the masses. They learn through actual suffering and kinstinctively recognise a leader. As Tilak's agitation now centred around a vital economic issue it touched them at once. Within the limits of law, Tilak did his best to make them self-reliant and his inspiring lead in effect went much beyond moderate demands of requests and petitions. His work was not merely negative but he showed great constructive ability. It was a common sight, according to the testimony of contemporaries, to see him going from shop to shop in the grain market of Poona requesting shopkeepers not to sell grains at too high price to the poor people. No wonder that the Government did not like this work of Sarvajanik Sabha and looked upon its work as a gross interference. The Anglo-Indian papers had already raised the cry of sedition and had accused Tilak of trying to start a no-rent campaign on the models of Irish no-tax campaign.[18]

Tilak also provided an insight into the causes of the famine. He pointed out that it was because Indian trade was monopolised by Britain, that the pressure on land had increased and agriculture was made unproductive. The officials were also too highly paid. He said, "It is true that lack of rain causes famine, but it is also true that the people of India have not the strength to fight the evil. The poverty of India is wholly due to the present rule. India is being bled till only the skeleton remains... all the vitality of the people is being sapped and we are left in an emaciated state of slavery." Tilak sent two petitions to the Government urging immediate relief to the people in the famine-stricken areas.

Nursing the Plague-Stricken

As Tilak had foreseen, the Government looked for an opportunity to gag him and it came as soon as the catastrophe of the plague set in. Tilak did not spare himself and did his best to help plague committee. It was mainly as a result of the lead taken by him that a Plague Hospital for Hindus was built in Poona. He stayed in the town during the worst days of the epidemic and condemned the "educated leaders" who ran away as soon as the epidemic became severe.[19]

On the 9th March, two military officers were appointed to the committee to help Rand and then the real trouble started. The tone of Tilak's articles in the Kesari too changed and he referred to the "Havoc caused in Poona". In an article in Kesari of the 16th March, 1897, Tilak expressed mild resentment at the employement of the soldiers: "We do not understand why these soldiers have been brought. There was no reference to them in the Governor's speech. In Bombay they have not been employed. We believe that this idea must have originated from some subordinate official..." Yet, he was liberal enough to pay a compliment to the soldiers, "Though the soldiers have come it is gratifying to note that they are behaving in an orderly manner." Referring to the complaints made against the soldieres that they had polluted the deities by entering the houses, Tilak is more disposed to blame the 'native gentlemen', who accompany them; for it is natural, according to him, that the soldiers do not understand the customs of the Hindus but it is the native gentlemen who should guide them. He goes a step further and says that these search parties were unnecessary. "Had the Government only passed an order that anyone who does not report a patient would be punished all this trouble would have been averted." Letters from citizens of Poona complaining against the indiscretion of the soldiers were published in Kesari and they make it quite clear that the people were exasperated beyond expression by the plague administration. In a memorandum written to the committee, prominent citizens of Poona made several serious complaints about the misbehaviour of the soldiers.[20]

The vernacular press, headed by Kesari, cried itself hoarse and was termed seditious and disloyal. Fair-minded English journals, such as Daily News (London) and Manchester Guardian, were quick to lay the blame at the doors of the indiscretion of the Government in employing European soldiers.[21] Matters reached a crisis and the nerves of the people of Poona were on edge. Tilak sounded a note of warning; but among other things he also wrote certain things not directly connected with the plague, but which later were construed to have led to the murder of European officers. Tilak was presiding over a lecture by Prof. Bhanu on Shivaji. Prof. Bhanu had referred to the killing of Afzal Khan and had already propounded in an article contributed to the 'Deccan College Quarterly' in April 1896. In his speech, as reported in the Kesari of the 15th June 1897, Tilak said, "There is no need to find out new historical information regarding the assassination of Afzal Khan. Let us proceed on the assumption that Shivaji killed Afzal Khan by a preconceived plan. The question-is this act of the Maharaja good or bad?- is to be faced not from the standpoint of the Penal Code, nor of the Smritis of Manu and Yajnavalkya, nor is it to be considered inthe light of moral principles enunciated by both occidental and oriental systems. Laws regarding the regulation of society are for the observance of us common people. Great men are above the common principles of (Shastra) Law. In killing Afzal Khan, did Shivaji sin? The answer of this question is in Mahabharat itself. In the Bhagwatgita Shri Krishna has counselled the assassination of even one's elders and blood-relations. There is no blame when you do actions without wishing for their fruit. Maharaja did nothing in order to further his own interest.

He killed Afzal Khan with a righteous object of the public good. If thieves enter one's house, and one's wrists have no strength to drive them out, one may without compunction shut them in and burn them standing. God Almighty did not give a charter engraved on a copper plate to the foreigner (Mlenchha) to rule India. The Maharaja strove to drive them out of his fatherland, and there is no sin of covetousness in that."[22]

On June 30, 1897, Tilak wrote to the Times clarifying his position and explaining the nature of his work, under the caption "Sedition or Prejudice".[23] According to Tilak, the continued malicious remarks about him and the journals published by him compelled him to write the letters. He expected the Times to be at least fair; but it had grossly misrepresented the matter. He goes on to explain how he had supported 'stringent measures' and had also urged upon 'the leaders of the people' to assist the Government. He had called upon them to form committee to work for the people-his slogan being 'Do not complain but work'. If this is sedition, he says, then the Aglo-Indian vocabulary must be more comprehensive than the common English.

As for his own share in the work, Tilak organized Plague Committees, started a Plague Hospital and gave meals at cheap rates to the people. It is unjust to say that he or his paper only excited feelings of disaffection among the people. It should be appreciated that Tilak could not shut his eyes to complaints and grievances which he knew from personal knowledge to be well founded. Unnecessary stringency of the plague measures and not the writings of the Native Press were, according to him, responsible for the feelings of dissatisfaction. He pathetically bemoaned, "... it is extremely foolish to ignore all the work done by individuals and the good sense and the patience of a community as a whole, simply because a fanatic took it into his head to perpetrate a horrible deed, which, as I have said above, all of us equally deplore. Further discussion must, I think, be reserved for cooler times, when we shall be ready to look at men and things with unjaundiced eyes." Tilak also wrote three articles on the occasion of Queen Victoria's Jubilee in the Kesari entitled "Glory to Her Majesty the Queen Empress". They are in his usual mixed strain. He gave due credit to the British, but at the same time, utilized this occasion to ventilate the grievances of the people.[24]

The Weavers Guild

Another of Tilak's important constructive activities for the direct amelioration of the condition of the backward classes was the help he gave tothe weavers of Sholapur District. There were a number of weaver families there, who during the famine were given the manual labour of rubble breaking. The daily wages that they got in return were too inadequate to support them and Tilak pointed out that it was cruel and inhuman to make a craftsman class do such work. The Famine Code had stipulated that such craftsmen should be provided with capital, yarn, looms and other accessories to carry on their craft. Tilak suggested to the Government to give effect to those provisions to which vague replies were given and the bureaucracy showed the usual recalcitrance to move. Tilak thereupon sought the co-operation of the rich merchants of Sholapur and with their help he arranged to supply yarn to the weavers on a co-operative basis and also took guarantees for the sale of the cloth produced by the weavers. This resulted in the establishment of a weavers Guild. Owing to this guild, the weaver families could get enough work during the famine and even afterwards. As they carried on their activities on lines chalked out by Tilak they improved their condition to such an extent that the famine of 1900 had no terrors for them. Those people, therefore, left their petty labouring jobs and became independent and prosperious craftsmen, Tilak, therefore, became very famous among members of this class. It was estimated that the work brought relief to more than one thousand families comprising a total of about four to five thousand persons.[25]

The Vedokta Episode

The Vedokta episode is chronologically of a much later date-1901 - but it also shows the discriminating attitude adopted by Tilak in matters of social reform. The issue was whether to extend the privilege of Vedic rites to non-Brahmins. Tilak was not against it but he opposed the compulsion on Brahmin priests :

> "The question was whether an orthodox Brahmin should be coerced against his wish, on pain or forfeiture of inams granted to him under the old system to perform Vedic rites in all non-Brahmin families. The very principles of personal liberty would be violated, if we answer the question in the affirmative. I know that every community can freely resort to Vedokta rites if it chooses, but no one can justify the forfeiture of ancient inama granted by old rulers under a different understanding."

Tilak refused to go to the whole hog with the reformers and pulled them up frequently, but this does not imply that he was blind opponent of social progress. He had the insight to separate the chaff from the grain.[26]

Arbitrator in Conflicts Between Brahmins and Non-Brahmins

The Congress-League Pact had succeeded in bringing together the Hindus and the Muslims on the common platform of political rights; but now the non-Brahmin classes were clamouring for their rights. They constituted a separate group and when the Home Rule memoranadum was sent to Mongauge, they declared themselves aloof and distinct from the demands of the more advanced classes. At the Belgaum District conference in 1917. The dissension between the Brahmins and non-Brahmins had taken an acrimonious turn and Tilak, when questioned about it, said, "It is natural that the non-Brahmins should be angry with us. How could the enemies of the Congress sit still and quietly look on the unity forged at Lucknow between the Hindus and the Muslims? We have achieved this by granting special representation to the Muslims. Now the enemies of the Congress have raised up another bogey of disruption. But in one sense I am also happy that the simple minded non-Brahmins have started demanding certain things for themselves although out of spite for us at present. This shows a growth of self-confidence. Today the Government might concede to their demands to sow seeds of disruption among us; but gradually as the demands go on increasing, Government will have to disappoint them and this disappointment will make them join us. If we can prove to the non-Brahmins by example that we are wholly on their side in their demands fromthe Government, I am sure that in times to come their agitation, now based on social inequality, will merge into our struggle. Unless this happens, their movement will peter out in a short time."[27]

Now this statement of Tilak shows how practical and clear-sighted he was. He had a very keen understanding of forthcoming days; and this is why, his ideas were always different from others. A section of the non-Brahmins, under the leadership of Vithal Ramji Shinde, organized a Nationalist non-Brahmin Association in Poona. A public meeting was convened on the 8th November 1917 and was addressed by members of many backward communities. Tilak was called uponto speak on behalf of the Brahmin community and he readily agreed. In his speech he declared that they wanted a Swaraj not of the old type but on the Western pattern. It was because of the dissensions among the different castes that the British entrenched themselves in India and if these were to continue, Indians would remain equally backward even under Swaraj. Shinde said that he had occasion to test Tilak's alleged partiality to political reform and his indifference to social reform. When Shinde asked him whether he should give up his work among the depressed classes and devote himself exclusively to politics, Tilak said, "No" and in their free and frank talk afterwards, says Shinde, he was convinced that Tilak was wholly on the side of Depressed Class Mission in his individual capacity as Tilak, though not as the editor of the Kesari.

Writing in the Kesari on the 18th September 1917, Tilak tried to analyse the causes of dissensions between the Brahmins and non-Brahmins. He pointed out that it was inconceivable that the leaders of the non-Brahmins, being themselves educated, should subscribe to the present despotic rule. "Love of freedom being the greatest virtue of English education, all educated people, whether Brahmins or non-Brahmins, will not countenance the present stunted growth of the national talent for ever. The non-Brahmins are showing their self-confidence in their struggle against what appears to them to be social injustice. This same feeling must be shown in the political field also. It is natural for the non-Brahmins to wish for higher posts in the Government and more rights for themselves. It is not therefore possible that they would strike at the root of the demand for Swaraj."[28]

Having settled the first question that the non-Brahmins could not be opposed tothe demand of Swaraj as such, the next question, says Tilak, is the question of their demand for certain safeguards." This question the Brahmins are willing to consider not only sympathetically but generously too..." Tilak himself said at Lucknow that he would not mind if in the councils, none but a non-Brahmin is elected, because he wanted a majority of Indians there instead of the foreigners. "The general policy of the Brahmins towards the non-Brahmins would be the same as that of Hindus towards the Muslims; there should therefore be no apprehension on that account. The Brahmins have never said that they want all the seats in the councils. The fact that they get more seats than what are due to them according to their population is because of their advance in education. It is a totally false allegation that the Brahmins had put the non-Brahmins and other castes down by purposely denying them the facility of education. It is doubtful if the four-class system was prevalent in its entirety any time in the past. Even if it were and even if the rights of education, sacrifice and acceptance of gifts were reserved for the Brahmins, their extent was very limited. Education was necessary for everyday life and the literacy required for it were withinthe reach of all, including the Shudras. Excepting the learning of the Vedas, what we call education today, was easily available to all. Even then the three classes remained aloof from education because they paid more attention to their professions and neglected their education. They profited therefore in point of monetary gains, just as the Brahmins profited in point of learning. The Brahmins do not, however, complain that the other classes kept them poor, just as the non-Brahmins complain today that the Brahmins kept them ignorant. Today the Brahmins do not stand in the way of the non-Brahmins getting their education but are, on the contrary, prepared to help them. Even then non-Brahmins do not come forward to take bookish education. The Government is sympathetic towards the non-Brahmins, and yet, looking to the convenience of the administration, they have appointed Brahmins to higher posts and also nominated them to the councils. This was because the Brahmins were educated while the non-Brahmins were not."

Tilak, therefore, argued that the true distinction was not between the Brahmins and non-Brahmins, but between the educated and the non-educated. It is the educated of any caste, who would get the higher privileges. About the question of communal representation, Tilak said that, though nationally he was not favourable to it, he was not opposed to anyone who wanted it. The true eligibility for voting and representation should be a minimum educational standard and an income level and not considerations of caste and community.[29]

Thus, according to Tilak, the problem was not of Brahmins and non-Brahmins but it was the problem of educated and non-educated. He was against the communal or caste representation. We, the people of modern times, are bound to praise this healthy idea of Tilak, because we are facing a grave crisis today due to this caste and community representation. The caste and community struggles are growing fast in these times and the problem is becoming hard and harder and at the root of all these problems is lack of real education. Tilak was clear-sighted enough to visualize the far-reaching consequence of his agitation for independence. particularly as it was bound to usher in an era of ameliorating the conditions of the downtrodden. More than once he described his political idea as "the Swaraj of oilmen and sellers of betel-nut leaves", by which he meant the toiling masses, irrespective of caste and creed. A close student of French philosopher Rousseau, and the Italian prophet of modern Europe, Mazzini, Tilak could not have failed to see that the political democracy of his dream must inevitably lead to social and economic equality.

At this stage we quote an extract from Tilak's reply to Dr. R.P. Paranjpe, who had attacked him for refusing signature to a manifesto condemning untouchability :
"Paranjpe knows full well that I am for removing all caste distinctions regarding interdining and untouchability. I have said so many a time, but I am not prepared to take up the work of actual propaganda in this matter, as many know, and I refuse to sign a manifesto which would have clearly thrown that responsibility on me." Herein lies the essence of Tilak's opposition to the social reformers.[30]

An episode, which took place in 1890, throws some interesting light both on the social condition in India hundred years ago and on the fighting spirit of Tilak. On this occasion he became not the ideal of the orthodox section of the community, but its most hated victim. Today it may sound silly, but in those days it was something of a storm in a tea-cup. However, to pacify his angry followers, Tilak did undergo a sort of penance and there the episode ended. Here lay the fundamental difference between Tilak and other social reformers. He wanted to take the people with him and was therefore extremely careful, not to hurt their religious feelings. He pointed out that social reformers would never succeed by ridiculing the age-old customs and habits of the people which were hallowed by long practice and tradition. When his progressive opponents quoted the example of Luther, who reformed the Christian faith, he neatly turned the tables on them by pointing out, "Luther succeeded because he believed and respected the tenets of Christianity. He did not flout the Bible. Let our reforming friends follow the great Christian leader and respect the Hindu scriptures and they will see a miraculous change in the attitude of the people."

The secret of Tilak's hold onthe masses lay in his deeply-held respect for the religion of his forefathers. All that was ancient and truly noble in Hindu tradition was sacred to him. Indeed, his profound reverence for the knowledge of the Vedas was his sheet anchor amid all the social and religious upheavals of his day, which only too easily became tempestuous storms at the slightest change in the atmosphere.[31]

Tilak's opponents accused him of hypocrisy and chicanery but the charge is not correct. His stands must be seen in the socio-political set-up of the time. K.V. Godbole has correctly pointed out that Tilak's opposition to social reform was more apparent than real. He was sensitive to social evils and injustice and would never have tolerated them in a free India. He granted to the emancipation of the country the first priority in his national programme for he believed that without it, social reform could make no real headway.[32]

Not an Orthodox

On the basis of the above survey of Tilak's social stands, we can say that the charges of orthodoxy on Tilak do not appear to be true. Tilak was neither a hypocrite nor a mere platform reformer. He practised what he preached. His social creed can be best summed up in his own words from the famous rejoinder he gave to R.P. Paranjpe in the columns of the Bombay Chronicle an year before his death: "I do not hold that social reconstruction must be undertaken prior to political emancipation. I attach much greater importance to the latter. Without the power to shape our destiny, our national regeneration cannot, in my opinion, be effected and I have throughout my career tried to preachand emphasize these views. When I opposed the Age of Consent Bill, I did so mainly on this ground. I did not think, nor do I think now, that a legislature, which is not wholly responsible to the public, is competent to deal with social questions."[33]

Regarding his alleged opposition to the social reform movement Tilak wrote: "A true nationalist desires to build on old foundation. Reform based on utter disrespect for the old does not appeal to him as constructive work. He, therefore, tries to maintain and foster a distinctive national interest before undertaking any reform. A similar change has come over Irish politics... We don't want to Anglicise our institutions and so de-nationalise them in the name of social reform. We mean to progress and wish our country to occupy a position of equality among the civilized nations of the world"[34]

After the Tea party incident Tilak comments : "The reformers want to bring about social reform with a magic wand. We think tha treform scan be brought about in conformity with the spirit of the time sand the environment. We all have families and want to live with society. Under these circumstances compromises willl alone endure. Those who only want to live according to their own individual whims should do so on a desert island. Others who want to live in society will have to follow a path of compromise."[35] Tilak's concept of social leadership stands on real and practical foundations. We can not accuse him of orthodoxy if we appreciate his true zeal for social reform without being unnecessarly idealistic or modernized.

Footnotes

1. N.G. Jog, *Lokamanya Bal Çangadhar Tilak*, Delhi, Government of India, Publication Division, p. 23.
2. *Ibid*, p. 29.
3. *Ibid*, p. 25-26.
4. Tahmankar, *op. cit.*, p. 42-43.
5. *Ibid*, p. 43-44
6. *Ibid*, p. 44-45
7. *Ibid*, p. 46
8. *Ibid*, p. 46-47
9. *Ibid*, p. 47
10. *Ibid.*
11. Jog, *op. cit*, p. 25.
12. *Ibid.*, p. 32-33.
13. Tahamankar, *op. cit.*, p. 49.
14. *Ibid.*, p. 49-50.
15. G.P. Pradhan and A.K. Bhagwat, *Lokamanya Tilak: A Biography*, Bombay, Jayco Publishing House, p. 100.
16. *Ibid.*
17. *Ibid.*, p. 101.
18. *Ibid.*, p. 102.
19. *Ibid.*, p. 104.
20. *Ibid.*, p. 105.
21. *Ibid.*, p. 105.
22. *Ibid.*, p. 106.
23. *Ibid.*
24. *Ibid.*, p. 107.
25. *Ibid.*, p. 101.
26. Jog, *op. cit.*, p. 29.
27. Pradhan and Bhagwat, *op. cit.*, p. 292.
28. *Ibid.*
29. *Ibid.*, p. 293.
30. Tahmankar, *op. cit.*, p. 50.
31. *Ibid.*, p. 52.
32. *Ibid.*, p. 321.
33. Jog, *op. cit.*, p. 30-31.
34. *Ibid.*, p. 31.
35. *Ibid.*, p. 28.

4 Political Bases of Tilak's Nationalism

Tilak made 'Swrajya' or 'Home Rule' his absolute goal, because he characterized the English Government in India as an "alien" government. In his speech at Ahmednagar, he said, "The English Government was as a matter of fact alien, and there was no sedition whatever nor any other offence in calling alien those things which are alien."[1] Referring to the meaning of alien, he said: "By alien I do not mean alien in religion. He who does what is beneficial tothe people of this country, be he a Muhammadan or an Englishman, is not alien. Alienness has to do with interests. Alienness is certainly not concerned with white and black skin. Alienness is not concerned with religion. Alienness is not concerned with trade and profession. I do not consider him an alien who wishes to make an arrangement whereby that country in which he has to live, his childern have to live and his future generation have to live, may see good days and be benefited. He may not perhaps go with me to the same temple to pray to God, perhaps there may be no intermarriages and interdining between him and me. All these are minor questions. But if a man is exerting himself for the good of India, and takes measures in that direction, I do not consider him an alien. The Government is alien. At first I thought that there was nothing particular in this. The Peshwa's rule passed away and the Muhammadan rule passed away, the country came into the possession of the English, but the King's duty is to do all these things whereby the nation may become eminent, be benefitted, rise, and become the equal of other nations. That King who does this duty is not alien. He is to be considered alien, who does not do this duty, but looks only to his own benefit, to the benefit of his own race, and to the benefit of his original country. If anybody has charged this government with being alien, he has done so in the above sense."[2] Tilak's concept of alienness thus coincides with that of colonialism and he wanted to attain 'Swaraj' to get rid from this alienness or colonialism.

Tilak was not a platform politician. He was a man of action and he knew that without the unification of the country and political consciousness of the people, Swaraj will remain only like a day's vision. So he worked steadfastly to create political bases for his vision of nationalism.

Shivaji Festival

Tilak wanted to give his political activities a national turn by arousing the sentiments of the people around a national hero. No better figure in Maratha history was so respected by all sections of the public like Shivaji. The forts standing in different parts of the Sahyadri ranges in Maharashtra were a living testimony of Shivaji and in Poona, as also in the part of the Deccan, a number of places were still remembered for their association with the exploits of Shivaji.[3]

Tilak was very explicit about the object of the Shivaji celebrations. To him, Shivaji was a national hero and at a time when national qualities of solidarity, patriotism, hatred of tyranny were absent, he wanted to make an appeal by invoking the memory of the glorious times of the great national hero. He said in a speech at Amraoti, "Every person should think about his town, his country, his community and the nation. He should ask himself the question whether the condition ofthe country is in a flourishing state or has decayed. If it is unfortunately the latter, he must try to find out means for its betterment. It is with this end in view that the Shivaji festival is being celebrated." He cited the example of the jubilee celebrated by the British and says that the jubilee celebration conjures up a picture of the growth of the empire inthe minds of the British. In these days in schools, there is the kindergarten system by which a clear idea is given of an object to the child by showing it to him. In the same way celebrations of heroes are object lessons by which ideas of national uplift are instilled in the mind of the people. According to Tilak, we have a number of religious festivals but we must have political celebrations. They will enable us to understand politics and we will also know the state which we are in.[4] Thus Tilak wanted children in India to be politically socialized through symbols of Indian unity and chivalry. In pursuance of this idea, he organized the first Shivaji celebration which was a great success and the villagers from all over Maharashtra had gathered at the place, some of them walking several miles.

Tilak continued to organize Shivaji festivals to arouse wider national consciousness and for the unification of country. In an English speech in Calcutta, where the Bengalees had picked up this idea of Shivaji celebrations, he was still more definite about the aims and objects of the Shivaji celebrations : "Human nature is so constituted that we cannot do without festivals. It is the nature of man to love festivals. We must have festivals. If you want to keep up your spirit, you should assemble once a year at least, and you should concentrate your intellectual and spiritual forces for a particular idea. The utsab were originated and celebrated simply to keep the memories of days gone by. Unfortunately we had no political festival tokeep up the memory of our heroes except the National Congress. This is the reason why the Shivaji festival was started in Maharashtra with the hope that it will spread all over India without distinction of caste and creed. There is no reason to object to the festival because Shivaji was a Mahratta, because the life of Shivaji was not up to the standard of the twentieth century. These are minor points. If Shivaji was a mahratta-it was because he was born at Poona. If you look at the ethnology you will find Shivaji belonged to the same stockof the Rajputana. You may call him a Rajput if you like and you may call him a Bengalee if you like. And therefore you should continue the celebrations from year to year. It is such an inspiring festival that in these days we cannot afford to do without it. The central idea is that you must take the spirit from the life of Shivaji. There had been various objections started not here but in my own province. Some objected to it because they were Mahomedans. That objection no longer exists. Shivaji did not fight against the Mahomedans but against the tyrannical power that existed at that time. There are instances in his career. A lieutenant of Shivaji had defeated a Mahomedan chief and his family was captured and was taken to Shivaji. Shivaji at once sent the lady to the private chamber and asked his lieutenant to send her back to her husband. That is the spirit in which you must read the life of Shivaji and if you read the life of Shivaji in the proper spirit, I can assure you that you are sure to derive an inspiration, a sentiment in life which will serve you in these days which you cannot draw from the history of any other country. Shivaji was essentially a man and that is the reason why we should celebrate his life. The Goddess Kali is the presiding deity in Bengal. The same Goddess was the protectress of Shivaji. We cannot conceive of Shivaji without Bhavani. His whole life was, as it were, engulfed and inseparable from Bhavani. And we cannot read of Shivaji without Dhavani."[5] Tilak wanted to attach the Bengalees with Shivaji at the sentimental level and with that end in view, he had referred tothe relation of Goddess Kali with Shivaji. But Tilak was not content with seeking the unity of regions alone through the symbol of Shivaji.

Tilak also wanted Muslims to take part in the Shivaji celebrations. He said in his same speech in Calcutta: "I do not mean to say that Mahomedans should come to worship the Goddess but surely they should take part in the festival just as we take part in the Mahomedan festival of Moharram in Poona. Abstaining from the worship is no reason why we should not take part in the festival itself. It is to give a corporal shape to our political ideas that we Hindus should have festivals like these. History tells us taht in the worst days of Mahomedan rule Mahomedans worshipped Shivaji with the same enthusiasm as the Hindus."[6]

In another article in the Mahratta, dated the 24th June 1906, he met some of the objections against the festival by saying, "Hero-worshipis a feeling deeply implanted in human nature and our political aspirations need all the strength which the worship of a Swadeshi hero is likely to inspire into our minds. For this purpose Shivaji is the only hero to be found in the Indian history. He was born at a time when the whole nation required relief from misrule; and by his self-sacrifice and courage, he proved to the world that India was not a country forsaken by Providence. It is true that the Mahomedans and the Hindus were then divided, and Shivaji, who respected the religious scruples of the Mahomedans, had to fight against the Mogul rule that had become unbearable to the people."[7] Tilak suggested that Shivaji was not against the Muslims, but he was against the Moghul rulers, because they were oppressive, tyrannical and despotic rulers. Tilak exhorted his Mohammedan listeners to pay no attention to the Anglo-Indian writers who were making a bogey of Shivaji festival and telling the people that the Mahratta hero was anti-Mohammedan. He asked them to accept Shivaji as one who "in his own days took a bold stand against the tyranny of his time."[8]

Tilak drew the analogy of Britain honouring Nelson and France worshipping Napolean without straining their mutual relations. He assured the Muslims, "The Shivaji festival is not celebrated to irritate you. Times are changed and the Mahommedans and the Hindus are inthe same boat so far as the political conditions of the people are concerned. Can we not both of us derive inspiration from the life of Shivaji under these circumstances?"[9]

It is important to note that some Muslims at least inthe beginning of the festivals, joined the celebrations together with the Hindus, which gives the direct lie to men like

Valentine Chirol, who asserted that Tilak had inaugurated the Shivaji cult as an anti-Muslim movement.[10]

Tilak turned his attention to organizing the enthusiasm of the people in secular matters. Like Thomas Carlyle and Emerson, he believed that the "heroes" are the creators of History. It is their great work which inspires the ordinary man, gives him ideals to aim at, and raises his moral stature. He believed that a community can only continue to live and prosper if it can produce an unbroken chain of great men to serve and inspire it. When it no longer throws up great men, the community declines and dies. This reasoning led him to the conclusion that the people must be given a hero to worship who would help them to rediscover their self-esteem and self-respect, without which they could never hope to make the supreme effort in self-secrifice for their political liberation.[11]

Tilak found in Shivaji a hero. He thought that Shivaji would be an acceptable figure to Brahmins and non-Brahmins alike, and the agitation for Swaraj would reach the masses more quickly than by any other means. In Maharashtra, Shivaji and Swarajya were the two sides of coin.[12] By 1906, this festival was being regularly celebrated in Banaras, Karanchi, Madras and in Calcutta, the capital city of Bengal which was supposed to have suffered at the hands of the Mahrattas. The people responded enthusiastically to this festival everywhere, the four corners of the country and each celebrated it with as much enthusiasm as in Poona.

The European community was quite unable to understand how a Mahratta leader like Tilak could be so enthusiastically received and heard with such rapt attention on his favourable theme of Shivaji by Bengali audiences sometimes numbering tens of thousands. Shivaji was the bogey man of Bengal, yet the magic of Tilak's name and his superbly logical way of explaining the life work of Shivaji, changed the old prejudice into warm affection and respect for the Mahratta hero. Bengalis accepted Shivaji as their own national hero and drew new inspirations from him. Ever since those days, bonds of sympathy and affection have bound together Maharashtra in the West and Bengal in the East. These two provinces stuck together throughout the national struggle from 1905 to 1947 and a unity of purpose and ideals was established which led to a union of minds. Bengal and Maharashtra began to think and act alike, whether it was over the programme of the New Party, the terrorist movement of secret societies or organized opposition of Mahatma Gandhi's programme of non-co-operation. As the sedition Committee said in its report "Any cult started in Maharashtra has its echoes at once in Bengal."[13]

Ganapati Festival

Tilak tried to use the religious fervour of the people for political purposes by celebrating the Ganapati festival. From his study of Greek history he had learnt how Olympian Games had developed into a great national festival which built up a national spirit among the many independent city states of Greece. Every fourth year, a religious festival in honour of god Jupiter was held in the plain of Olympia, with sacrifices, processions, and games while poets and authors recited their compositions and artists displayed their works. The Olympian Games thus gradually became a bond of union for all the Greeks, linking them together in peace and love of their country.[14]

In 1893, Tilak hit on the idea of giving a new direction to the already established forms of worship and started a revivalist movement. He found in the Ganesh festival a "powerful engine for imparting instructions to the masses" who were, he said, "our ultimate court of appeal".[15] In an article entitled "The Need of National Festival", Tilak refers to the part played by them in Greece and Rome. "In India, religion will always be regarded as of primary importance and as such our celebrations will naturally have a religious colour. Formerly such occasions were used for keeping the religious sense alive and to give ethical, social and political education to the people. In the time of Vedas, the great sacrifices were inthe nature of national celebrations. The risist gathered at the time of the sacrifices carried on discussions on ethical and religious problems. Such festivals were revived by saint Ramdas in the days of Shivaji. It is the duty of the educated people, therefore, to take an active part in these celebrations instead of lecturing on Bhakti or uttering the name of God behind closed doors."[16] When writing about the function of the Brahmin class in modern society, Tilak had spoken of the necessity on the part of the Brahmins to take up the work of social education by turning into missionaries. He called them 'Graduate Ramdas is' recalling how in the time of saint Ramdas a number of his disciples had wandered through the length and breadth of Maharashtra preaching the message of Hindu national revival under the Muslim rule.[17]

In another article in Kesari (8th September 1896) "The Ganesh Festival", Tilak is more explicit about his primary aim of channellizing the religious fervour of the people for political ends: "The aims of such national festivals are the two-fold aims of entertainment and public education. A nation fettered by the foreigners rarely sees such days of glory and happiness. Dassera was the only day of national rejoicing in Maharashtra, but today under a foreign yoke we cannot celebrate it in its true spirit. It is not again a new thing; religious festivals are age-old and our religious sentiments naturally surge up at their mere mention. They are ways devised by our ancestors to keep up the religious faith of the people, to vitalize the ethical and political life of the people and to keep the flame of our nationalism burning bright. The educated people, therefore, are betraying a sacred trust by not joining these festivals. Why should not these occasions be utilized for industrial exhibitios of indigenous products? Why should not the educated people use these fairs for the propagation of various ideas? After all this will not be as expensive as the National Congress. Besides, the educated persons can easily do here the work that can never be done by the Congress. Why should not these fairs be converted into huge meetings? Will not your political agitation enter the huts in the villages by these methods? Can you not spread the ethical and religious knowledge that you have acquired after a good deal of labour by these methods which are so easy and which cost so little? Why should not the educated people bring home to them the real state of the country? Why not those who call themselves wise, enlighten people about the tyranny of the Government? Or again why would they not strengthen our feelings of nationalism on the basis of religious faith?... There is no greater folly than considering the educated classes as different from society. The educated are after all a part and parcel of the society."[18]

Tilak's expectations were more than fulfilled, for the Ganapati celebrations were held in all parts of Maharashtra and the people from all communities took part in them. They provided one of the cheapest means of varied entertainment and besides they were used as a ground for political propaganda, as Tilak had envisaged. Its choirs of singers or melas, mostly recruited from the gymnasts, sang songs which had a political and ethical import. These songs did yeoman service in popularising Swadeshi and carried on effective propaganda for the anti-drink campaign/ as it normally happens it also developed certain obnoxious traits later, but at the time of its inception, it more than fulfilled the expectations of its promoters. He had succeeded in bringing together the masses through the Ganapati festival and had succeeded in modernizing them to a certain extent.[19]

Valentine Chirol wrote in his book 'India'.

> "Conscious of his growing power outside the Deccan, Tilak neglected no means of strengthening his hold on his own people. To the prestige of his high caste, he added an intimate familiarity with the habits of thought and speech of his Mahrattas, and he knew how to play on their religious emotions when he gave a new meaning to the cult of their favourite god,

> the elephant-headed Ganesh or Ganapati by making his festival the occasion of popular demonstration in which he grafted a new hatred of British rule on to the old hatred of Mohammedan domination, still kept burning fiercely in their folk-songs and semi-religious plays."[20]

An importnt feature of the festival, Tilak notes, is the enthusiasm shown by all castes and communities among the Hindus. He himself being essentially a man of masses has given a vivid description of the festival. He shows the jubilation of the promoter of a novel idea who sees the popular response that it has evoked. The great enthusiasm shown by all classes of people in the Ganapati festival, Tilak thought, was a fitting answer to the atheistic and anti-religious feelings let loose by the reformers. He said, "It is particularly gratifying to note that in spite of the propaganda of Christian missionaries and atheistic reformers the heart of the society, viz. the Marathas, were yet true to their religion."[21] After paying an enthusiastic tribute to the orderly manner in which the festival was celebrated in Poona and at other places, Tilak speaks about the wider importance of the celebration. According to him, such festivals are an important means of bringing about national unity. If people come together with the object of public worship their minds are moulded in a particular way and the sense of brotherhood for all fellowworshippers is developed. Once then the mind and the heart reach a particular state of culture it is possible to use them for other purposes as well. How can a person be proud of his country who does not feel proud of his religion? That is how religion and nationality are interconnected.[22]

In a recent analysis of Asian nationalism, an American writer, Willian Holland, has observed that religion played an important role in India, where the natioalist movement has been characterized by a strain of Hindu revivalism. Like all empires, the British suppressed political meetings but they observed a hands-off policy with regard to religion. This provided a loophole which nationalists like Tilak exploited to the full for their own purpose, and the revival of the Ganapati festival is an outstanding example. Victor Barnow, writing in the American Anthropologist of Feb. 1954 says, "First of all, he thought that a public ten-day festival would provide a good occasion for lectures and anti-British propaganda. Second, Tilak hoped that a public Ganapati festival would bring the Hindu community together vis-a-vis the Muslim and provide a sense of Hindu solidarity."[23]

There is an interesting point in favour of Tilak's selection of the Ganapati festival in preference to many other possible festivals in the Hindu calendar. This shows that Tilak, far from being enemical to the Muslim sentiments, was very considerate towards Muslim rituals. The climax of Ganapati festival was the immersion of the tabuts, which takes place at the end of the Muslim festival of Moharram. The Ganapati festival, being modelled on the Moharram, may appeal tothe Muslims. The report of the Sedition Committee (1918-19) however suggested that the Hindu procession and immersion of Ganapati, which are such a close parallel to the Muslim ceremony, were intended by Tilak as a deliberate insult to the Muslims. But it should also be observed that many Hindu festivals, such as those of Durga and Sarasvati, end in a similar way, with a procession and immersion.[24] Answering those people who thought that the procession of Ganapati is an imitation of Muharram Tilak observed:

> "Those who say that the procession of Ganapati is an imitation of the tabuts of Muslims have not seen the Bhajan clubs on the occasion of the Ekadashi of Asadh and Kartik. The playing of lezim, the beating of large drums and such other things are observed in every fair. For the last two or three hundred years, some of us even though professing the Hindu faith used to make vows to Muslim gods or heroes during the Muharram. It was because we saw God in all beings. But Muslims, forgetting our longstanding friendship, played into the hands of undesirable

people and began a regular campaign of harassing Hindu religious mendicants. That inevitably led to estrangement."[25]

"Religious thoughts and devotion", said Tilak, "may be possible even in solitude, yet demonstration and eclat are essential to the awakening of masses. Through this nationalist appeal, the worship of Ganapati spread from the family circle to the public square. The transition is noteworthy since (despite some exceptions) Hindu religious worship is largely a matter of individual or family worship. Congregational worship as that in Christianity or Islam is not common. But nationalism provided the necessary social cement in this case."[26]

Tilak said, "When we know that Christian ecclesiasts can make reference to controversial political matters from the pulpit, we do not see why the festival melawalas should be debarred from saying a thing or two about the political conditions that they see all around them. It will be seen, therefore, that there is not much wrong in principles if, occasionally, we find songs treating a subject not strictly religious. It is disingenuous to attack this essentially religious festival as a cloak for political education."[27]

National Education

For eradicating the evils of the society Tilak recommended national education. "Education and not legislation is the proper method for eradicating the evils", he had repeatedly averred. In his view, nothing can be possible without a proper kind of education. Education teaches a man to differentiate between good and evil. Because man cannot understand the difference between good and bad without education; they cannot think about themselves in a proper manner if they are not educated. Therefore, according to Tilak, education was the prime thing for the people of the country. But he was not satisfied with the system of education, introduced by British in India, because this education did not give students the knowledge of true condition of their country. According to Tilak, national education was necessary for the development of personality of the students.

In a speech at Barsi in 1908 he said, "To be able to read and write alone is no education. These are simply the means of its attainment. That which gives us knowledge of the experience of our ancestors is called education. It may however be through books or through anything else. Every business needs education and every man has thus to give it to his children. There is no business indeed which does not require education. Our industries have been taken away by other people, but we do not know it. A potter knows how to shape a pot of China clay but does not know what this clay is made of; hence his industry is lost."[28] In this very speech, Tilak put stress on the necessity of various kinds of education, "Similarly is the necessity of religious education. How can a person be proud of his religion, if he is ignorant of it? They want of religious education is one of the causes that brought the missionary influences all over our country. We did not think it until very lately whether we get this sort of education or not."[29] He pointed out that the tradesmen sent their sons very reluctantly to school and some of them do not send at all; because they do not get the education which they need. Besides, their sons educated in the present-day system turn out fashionable. They wish to become clerks. They feel ashamed to sit on the gaddi where their forefathers earned the whole of their estate. The reason of this is that the education which they receive is one-sided. The Government wanted engineers, doctors and clerks. It therefore started such schools which could supply its need. The students who came out of these schools at first were bent upon services. He averred that it was not the fault on the part of Indians that even after getting so much education they remain unable to satisfy their bare necessities; but the fault went direct tothe British system of education that they received. He therefore suggested reformin the then prevalent system of education.

He asked the Government to give Indians control over the selection of text-books for schools, and he wanted such text-books to be selected which prepared Indians to be good citizens. The Governor of Bombay also admitted the necessity of reforms in the present system of education. But he pleaded that the Government was short of funds. Tilak did not consider this excuse to be reasonable. The Government of Britain did not provide such education which may inspire patriotic sentiments amongst Indians. In America, the Proclamation of Independence is taught in V or VI classes. In this way, they train their children in politics. But Indians were neither provided training in their religiion nor in patriotism. Tilak wanted schools to be established in the villages. For proper education from all sides he said that national schools must be started. There are some of our private schools but owing to the fear of losing the grant-in-aid the necessary educatin was not given in schools. Hence he exhorted Indians to start their own schools for imparting proper education and to do this selflessly. He lauded efforts which were being made all over the country. The Gurukul of Hardwar stood on new footings. Berar and Madras had also begun to move in that direction. Maharashtra, he said, was a little backward in it. A few efforts were being made here also; but they needed encouragement from people. Money was greatly needed in that work. But he was sure that if people realised the necessity and importance of education, they would encourage the organisers generously.[30]

Tilak elaborated what the schools of national education would give priority to. Religious education would be their first preference. He said, "Of the many things that we will do there is the religious education will first and foremost engage our attention. Secular education only is not enough to build up a character. Religious eduction is necessary because the study of high principles keeps usaway from evil pursuits. Religion reveals to us the form of the Almighty. Says our religion that a man by virtue of his action can become even a God. If we can become Gods event, by virtue of action why may we not become wise and active by means of our action like the Europeans? Some say that religion begets quarrels. But I ask, "Where is it written in religion to pick up quarrels?" If there be any religion in the world which advocates toleration of other religious beliefs and instructs to stick toone's own religion, it is alone the religion of the Hindus. Hinduism to the Hindus while islamism to the Musalmans will be taught there to forgive and forget the differences of other religions."[31]

Critics have criticized the idea of religious education, but today we can say that Tilak was not so much wrong. Nowadays, the religious education is invoked to fill up the void left by the lack of ethical and moral values in the society. Modern secular education is producing only a machineman or a businessman who works only for his self-interest. This inculcated selfishness which has been increasing in the whole world in its worst form. In this environment, the only medicine may appear to be religious education to cure the selfish illness of human beings. Tilak continued in the same speech, "The second thing that we will do, will lighten the load of study of the foreign languages. In spite of a long stay in India no European speaks for a couple of hours fluent Marathi, while our graduates are required as a rule to obtain proficiency in the English language. One who speaks and writes good English is said, in these days, to have been educated. But a mere knowledge of the language is no true education. Such a compulsion for the study of foreign languages does not exist anywhere except in India. We spend twenty or twenty-five years for education which we can easily obtainin seven or eight years if we get it through the medium of our vernaculars. We cannot help learning English, but there is no reason why its study should be made compulsory. Under the Mahomedan rule we were required to learn the Persian but we were not compelled to study it. To save this unnecessary waste of time we have proposed to give education through our own vernaculars."[32]

The third item of Tilak's National education was industrial education. He said, "The industrial education will be the third thing. In no school this educatin is given. That will be given inthese schools. It is an important thing. During the whole of this century we did not know how a match is prepared. In Sholapur, matches are manufactured from straw; and straw is found abundantly in our country. If, therefore, this industry is taken into our hands, the importance of matches will largely decrease in India. It is sam ewith the sugar industry. We can procure here as good sugarcanes as are found in Mauritius. It is seen by scientific experiments that the sugarcanes found in the sugarcanes of Mauritius. Six crores of rupees are drained out every year from this country only for sugar. Why should this be? Well, can be not get here sugarcanes, or the machinery necessary for its manufacture? The reason is that we do not get here the education in this industry. It is not so in Germany. The Department of Industry investigates there as to which industry is decaying, and if perchance there be any in a decaying state, a substantial support at once comes forth from the Government for reviving it. The British Government, too, does the same thing in England. But our Government does not do it here. It may be a mistake or the Government may be doing it knowingly, but it is clear that we must not be silent if the Government is not doing the job."[33] He wanted that a large mechanical and scientific laboratory should be established inschools. "Sugar produces rab and from rab is extracted liquor, but the Government does not permit us this extraction, hence Indians did not get cheap sugar. Mauritius exported twenty thousand tons of sugar every year to India." All these things were due to the policy of the Government, but Indians did not know it. The Government will be obliged to change its policy if Indians put pressure upon it. He said, "We have come to learn these things not earlier than twenty-five years after leaving the college. Our youngmen should know them in their prime of life."[34]

Tilak gave the example of mechancial education of Germany: "Some eighty or ninety years ago the industries of Germany declined on account of the rivalry between England and that country. But the German Government at once started scientific and mechanical education in that country. In this way Germany became so powerful in commerce that she has now become an object of dread to other countries."[35]

Political education was also necessary for Tilak: "Education in politics will be the fourth thing. We are not taught this subject in the Government schools. The students must understand that the Queen's Proclamation is the foundation of our rights. The Government is trying to shut our young men from these things. What has been proved by our revered grand old man - Dadabhai Naoroji, after a ceaseless exertion for over fifty years, should be understood by our students in their youth. Every year some thirty or forty crores of rupees are drained out of India without any return. We have, therefore, fallen to a wretched state of poverty. These things, if understood in the prime of life, can make such a lasting impression over the hearts of our young men, as is impossible at an advanced age. Therefore, this education should be given in school."[36]

Thus, Tilak wanted a full-fledged educational system in which a student can get a real kind of education. National education was necessary to build national character. He wanted the Government to do something for this kind of education but at the same time, he exhorted that if the Government could not do it, Indians must do themselves. He had no doubt that Indians did not get this sort of national education for want of self-government. So he announced in his speech: "We should not therefore await the coming of these rights, but we must get up and begin the work."[37] Tilak did not only give this idea in his speeches, but fulfilled it in action also. He started the New English School Poona and Fergussion College Poona, which could be said to be the nursery of Indian nationalism.

National Language

Like the national education, national language was also very important according to Tilak, because a common language was necessary for the unity of linguistically divided India. He was the first Congress leader to suggest that Hindi, written in Devanagari script, should be the national language of India. During Curzon's regime the Kashi Nagari Pracharini Sabha, came out with a proposal that there should be a common script for all the Aryan languages, so that when a book was printed, it might be readily intelligible to all the people speaking Aryan languages. At a conference of the Nagari Pracharini Sabha, to which he was invited in December, 1905, he suggested that Devanagari should not only be the common script of all the Aryan languages, but also the script of national language. "A common script", he said, "is a part and parcel of the national movement; we must have a common language in the whole of India. If you want to draw a nation together, there is no force more powerful than a common language for all." Disintegration of the country in the past led inevitably to disintegration of the national language and to a consciousness of loyalty to regional languages. And when political unity was once again accomplished under British suzerainty, English assumed the place of India's national language. In Tilak's scheme, English had no place and he urged its replacement by Hindi. He anticipated that protagonists of various regional languages would advance the cause of their own scripts, but advised his countrymen to subordinate their local interests to the national necessity of a standard script. To Tilak the standardization of script was no less important than standardization of time and weight. There was no politics in it, and he asked Government to introduce in school books of each province a few lesson in the standard script so that the next generation became familiar with it from its early days. Like Lord Curzon's 'standard time', he said that "we want a standard script".[38]

Tilak had little time to organize a movement for the national language and common script, due to his engagement in public activities and the struggle for freedom, but he gave an idea which was very important for his successors. His approach was consiliatory, but he would make no compromise on the ultimate aim. His argument was : "The Bengalis naturally take pride in their own script. I do not blame them for it. There are others in Gujarat who say that their character is easy to write because they omit the head line. The Maharashtras on the other hand may urge that Marathi is the character in which Sanskrit is written and therefore, it ought to be the common character for the whole of India. I fully appreciate the force of these remarks. But we must come to a solution of the question and for that purpose, discuss the subject in a business like and practical manner." He said that whatever character would we adopt, it must be easy to write, elegant to the eye and capable of being written with fluency. The letters that would devise must be sufficient to express all the sounds in different Aryan languages, nay, must be capable fo being extended to express the Dravidian sounds without diacritic marks. There should be one letter for every sound and vice-versa and according to Tilak only the Devanagari was such and alphabet. As a political leader he came in contact with people of various provinces and could understand their tongue, but he could not read their books. "If a Bengali book", he said, "is printed in the Devanagari character, I can follow the author to a great extent, if not wholly, for over fifty per cent of the words used will be found borrowed or derived from Sanskrit." During his travels, he intensely felt the lack of a national language and often gave expression to this feeling. Addressing the Bharat Dharma Mohamandal at Banaras (Jan. 1906), he said, "I am sorry I cannot address you in any other language except Marathi and English. English should be boycotted for religious purposes. But I cannot help this now and hope you will excuse me."[39]

Tilak said that it was by a common language that we express our thoughts to others. Manu also said that everything is comprehended under or proceeded from Vak or language. But he was against the adoption of the Roman character, which was suggested by some as a way out of the conflicting claims of various Indian characters. He emphatifally asserted, "The suggestion appears to me to be utterly ridiculous. The Roman alphabet and Roman character are very defectiv and entirely unsuited to express sounds used by us. It has been found to be defective even by English grammarians." He claimed that even "European Sanskritists have declared that the Devanagari alphabet is more perfect than any which obtains in Europe."[40] Therefore, Tilak was very explicit about the national language, because a common language was necessary for the unification of the country and according to him the place of the national language could only be occupied by Hindi written in Devanagari script.

Hindu-Muslim Disputes

Tilak wrote a number of articles on the riots, which occured in different parts of the Bombay Presidency, during the period from 1890 to 1894. One of the riots occurred in Poona also. Tilak analysed the causes ofthe riots in his articles and suggested methods for establishing peaceful relationship between the two communities. He urged very strict measures to be taken against the rioters, and pointed out that the best way to bring about good understanding and unity among the two communities was to make them realise that each is capable of resisting any aggression by the other. Tilak always used to say that Muslims were not alien and they were living in India for centuries with Hinus. He said that both communities must realise that nothing was to be gained by these riots. So, he suggested both communities to live together peacefully. But he was against such people as Beck of Aligarh who tried to declare all Hindus as seditionists. He was against the policy of Muslim appeasement of the Government. Writing on the question of Hindu-Muslim riots,

Tilak strongly criticized the Government's partiality to the Muslims. Tilak raised one question: was it proper to punish the Hindus along with Muslims when it was evident, the Muslims were the original aggressors and that the Hindus had retaliated in self-defence.[41]

He made his point of view quite clear: "In this affair, just as there is a Hindu and a Muslim party, so there is a Government party as well. It must not be forgotten that this is a triangular fight. Both the communities must be allowed to observe their social and religious festivals without let or hindrance, and it is the duty of the Government to help the communities to carry them out without interference from either side. If a Hindu in his religious zeal enters a Muslim locality to save the life of a cow he must be punished for his excess of zeal. In the same way, Muslims who object to the playing of music by the Hindus on the occasion of certain religious festivals must also be punished."[42]

Writing on August 15th, 1893, he bluntly said: "The Muslims have assumed a boorish and arrogant attitude which is the result of the encouragement they receive from the Government. The British are never tired of telling the people that it is the presence of the English alone which protects the Hindus from the Muslims, an observation which adds to the arrogance of the latter. The real dispute is not between the educated leaders of the two communities; it is to be found among the uneducated and the illiterate. If such people are to be kept under control, the Government must abandon the policy of favouring one at the cost of the other. The rigours of law must be applied to both, equally and impartially. If the policy of strict neutrality is not observed by the Government, then the Hindus will have to fight in self-defence as they did in Bombay."[43]

Tilak clarified that he hated communal riots and that he had no intention of hurting the feelings of his countrymen but he added that "the Hindus must never forget that friendship and good relations can exist only between people of equal strength."[44] Tilak wanted the Hindus to develop their strength. Since Tilak exhorted the Hindus to gain strength, a number of British and Indian critics characterized him anti-Muslim.

Valentine Chirol wrote in his book 'Indian Unrest' : "In 1893 some riots in Bombay of a more severe character than usual gave Tilak an opportunity of broadening the new movement by enlisting in its support the old anti-Mohammedan feeling of the people. He not only convoked... meetings in which his fiery eloquence denounced the Mohammedans as the "Anti-Cow Killing Society", which was intended and regarded as a direct provocation to the Mohammedans who, like ourselves, think it no sacrilege to eat beef." The Anglo-Indian Press also misrepresented Tilak as a bigoted Hindu leader dreaming of the Mahratta Empire. Newspapers like the Times of India (Bombay) and the Pioneer (Allahabad) were his worst calumniators and carried vendetta against him to even absurd lengths. This was bound to have some effect on half-educated Muslim youths and even on some so-called constitutional leaders among the Hindus. But the thoughtful Muslims were not taken in by such kind of propaganda. They showed an awareness of the situation and some of them acted towards Tilak in a spirit of understanding.[45] Two instances of their attitude both of which happened at the time of his arrest and trial in 1897 show what their real feelings were. First, Justice Ranade refused, but Justice B. Tyabji allowed Tilak to be released on bail. Not only did the latter order Tilak's release on bail, but if it had been in his power he would have quashed the case there and then.[46] Secondly, when Tilak's friends were collecting funds for his defence in Bengal, the first and biggest amount of Rs. 7000 came from the Muslim business firm of Hajee Ahmed Hajee Hossain Hajee Abdul. In a covering letter, Hajee Ahmed wrote : "The moment the Government arrested him, Mr. Tilak ceased to be a leader of the Hindu community. He is now above all castes, creeds and religions. He is going to be prosecuted for his fight for India, the common motherland of the Muslim and Hindus."[47]

Conclusion

Tilak was not anti-Muslim. He wanted a strong Hindu community, but this desire of Tilak was an offshoot of Government's policy of encouraging Muslims to stand against the Hindus. Tilak opposed the partial policy of British government. As a leader of deep-insight, he knew that this was the starting point of 'divide and rule' policy of British government. This is why, he used to say that there wer three parties concerned in the Hindu-Muslim disputes. These three parties were the Hindus, the Muslims and the British government, and he thought that until the Government did not give up the partial policy, the two communities would never feel safe and sure about their position. Tilak's protest against the selfish policy of British government and his devotion to organizing the Hindus and making them strong, was not against Muslims, but it was a policy to oppose the wrong and selfish policy of British government. Time proved how right Tilak was when the British government divided the Bengal in 1905, and their 'divide and rule' policy came to light.

The two festivals that Tilak started for igniting nationalism and unity also account for his characterization as anti-Muslim and anti-government. The national importance of Shivaji and Ganesh festivals was explained by Tilak in two special articles in the Kesari on 1st and 8th September 1896. In this connection he referred to the Olympic festivals of Greece in which all sections of Greeks participated and which the Tara festival occupied in Ireland. The Independence Day celebrations in the United States of America, he said, were also meant to sustain the national consciousness amongst the Americans. These festivals covered the long period of his political career, in which he is seen to be directing all his energies towards re-awakening the people and preparing them for a sustained fight against the British rule. Some of the arm-chair politicians were frankly contemptuous of any contact with the masses, and called Tilak "a leader of oilmen and betel-nut sellers", meaning the common men of Idnia, the workers and the peasants. But in the Ganapati and Shivaji festivals, Tilak could claim to have brought the rich and the poor together in a common struggle to reach the goal of Indian liberation.[48]

Tilak said: "Here, in India, as religion occupied a vital place in the life of the people, our festivals normally assumed in the past a religious character; but the object was essentially to keep the religious instinct of the people alive and in addition the occasions were utilized as a means of educating the people inthe moral, social and political spheres... In brief a national festival is one of the principal means of the all-around development of the Nation."[49]

Tilak called upon the educated people particularly to take a leading part in the organistion of such festivals. According to him: "This work is not as strenuous or expensive as the work of the Congress, but the educated people can achieve results through these national festivals, which it would be impossible for the Congress to achieve. Will it not be possible for political activities to enter the humblest cottage of the villages through these festivals? Will it not thus be possible to make available to our illiterate countrymen in the villages the moral and the religious education which you have got after strenuous efforts? Our ancestors have created natural opportunities for people to get together. But for our educated people, these opportunities are as nothing. They are proud of the fact that they are educated. Their main difficulty is how to mix with the people... There is no greater folly than the educated people thinking themselves to be a different class from the average society. The educated belong to the people. They can only swim or sink with the people. They cannot be without society... We, therefore, request that the educated people should realise their duty in this matter and act accordingly."[50] Tilak thought that the educated people are the backbones of the society, and this is why he wanted more and more people to be educated. For this purpose, Tilak gave great importance to the subject of national education as part of national regeneration. Tilak expressed himself about the need of national education, both in the Kesari, as also in the public meetings, and his main aim was that the purpose of national education was rousing in the minds of the students a spirit of sound nationalism and patriotism.

Tilak decried the unnecessary emphasis on learning of English. He said that "One who speaks and writes good English is said in these days educated." But he drew attention tothe fact that it was always difficult to learn an alien language. He said that "In spite of a long stay in India no European speaks a couple of hours fluent Marathi; while our graduates are required as a rule to obtain proficiency in English language." Instead, Tilak emphasized the use of national language. If adequate attention would have been paid since then on the development of a national language, a national language would have developed and it would have been easier and faster for boys and girls to learn science and other subjects in their national language. English lovers argue that every kind of progress cannot be possible without English. We can cite the example of Russia and Japan where English was totally neglected, but they developed economically and technically. This may be possible in India also but for this we have to follow the path of national education shown by Tilak.

Footnotes

1. B. G. Tilak, *Speeches of Bal Gangadhar Tilak,* Madras, R. Thirumalai & Co., p. 114.
2. *Ibid.* p. 174-75.
3. Pradhan and Bhagwat, *op. cit.,* p. 81.
4. *Ibid.* p. 89.
5. Tilak, Speeches, *op. cit.,* p. 98-100.
6. *Ibid.* p: 99-100.
7. Pradan and Bhagwat, *op. cit.,* p. 90
8. Tahmankar, *op. cit.,* p. 65.
9. Jog, *op. cit.,* p. 49.
10. Tahmankar, *op. cit.,* p. 65.
11. *Ibid.* p. 63.
12. *Ibid.* p. 64.
13. *Ibid.* p. 66.

14. *Ibid.*, p. 60-61.
15. *Ibid.*, p. 61.
16. Pradhan and Bhagwat, *op. cit.*, p. 85.
17. *Ibid.*, p. 85.
18. *Ibid.*, p. 86.
19. *Ibid.*, p. 87.
20. Chirol, *op. cit.*, p. 99-100.
21. Pradhan and Bhagwat, *op. cit.*, p. 84-85.
22. *Ibid.*, p. 85.
23. Tahmankar, *op. cit.*, p. 62.
24. *Ibid.*, p. 63.
25. Jog, *op. cit.*, p. 44.
26. *Ibid.*, p. 44-45.
27. *Ibid.*, p. 45.
28. Tilak, Speeches, *op. cit.*, p. 120.
29. *Ibid.*
30. *Ibid.*, p. 122.
31. *Ibid.*, p. 123.
32. *Ibid.*, p. 123-24.
33. *Ibid.*, p. 124.
34. *Ibid.*, p. 125.
35. *Ibid.*, p. 121.
36. *Ibid.*, p. 125.
37. *Ibid.*, p. 126.
38. Ram Gopal, *Lokamanya Tilak: A Biography*, Bombay, Asia Publishing House, 1956, p. 240-41.
39. *Ibid.*, p. 241-42.
40. *Ibid.*, p. 242.
41. Tahmankar, *op. cit.*, p. 54.
42. *Ibid.*, p. 55.
43. *Ibid.*, p. 55-56
44. *Ibid.*, p. 56.
45. *Ibid.*, p. 57
46. *Ibid.*
47. *Ibid.*
48. *Ibid.*, p. 66.
49. D.P. Karmarkar, *Bal Gangadhar Tilak: A Sttudy*, Bombay, Popular Book Depot, p. 77.
50. *Ibid.*, p. 78.

5 Tilak and the Bureaucracy

Tilak's ideas of nationalism also cover his approach to bureaucracy. Confronted as he was with the British bureaucracy, it was natural that he should be absolutely against the bureaucracy under the British regime. Out of the total of 339 articles in the three volumes of his political writings covering 1795 pages, Tilak wrote 239 articles on bureaucracy, administration and related themes with approximately two-third of the total space.[1] That shows that he considered bureaucracy as a pivot of administration. Since under the British, bureaucracy represented colonial oppression, he saw the necessity of opposing the bureaucracy of the country. He said before the court at the time of his historic trial of 1908, about his articles : "You have the articles before you and as I told you these articles have been written in the course of a controversy which is an old one - a struggle between the bureaucracy and the people of this country. Here is a book in my hand. It gives proceedings of the Sarvajanik Sabha and the East India Association in the time of late Rao Saheb Mandalik. From all these you will find that this controversy has been going on ever since the year 1860."[2] The bureaucracy and the Government, both, were different things according to Tilak and the controversy with the bureaucracy was an old thing for the Indians. He said, "I do not want to say that whenever I quote a book I feel every sentiment and accept every argument stated therein. In quoting them I wanted only to show that the controversy is not a new one and that it has been carried on for the past thirty or forty years and that I am not entirely responsible for the views expressed in my articles. The bureaucracy is not the Government. It is likely to be urged, 'take away the bureaucracy and what hope is left?' The correct way for a British colony is not to be governed by a bureaucracy, there are other ways."[3]

Tilak cited the example of Professor Amon, who says in his book on Politics : "Nevertheless the case is more clear in respect of countries like British India, in which, through a series of fortuitous circumstances, England has been called to govern a population of alien race, language and customs out of all numerical proportion to the English residing in the country. In such a case the duties of Government can neither be ignored nor resigned nor transferred. They are a trust for a coming generation and for a new age. Every opportunity must be taken, as it is being taken in practice more and more, to habituate the native population to be the duties of self-government and to prepare them for a time when the imposed and alien rule can be first relaxed, then shared and finally withdrawn."[4]

Tilak was charged for sedition by the British government, because he wrote several articles in his paper Kesari against the bureaucarcy, such as : 'The Country's Misfortune', 'A Double Hint', 'The Secret of the Bomb', 'These Remedies are not Lasting' and 'Chapter of Sins'. Referring to his charged articles he said, "It is not a question of the very existence of Government, but the form of Government. I have already referred you to what Major Evan Bell says on the subject and that is exactly what Lord Morley says. The question does not touch the existence of Government. The bomb outrages were quickly condemned in my paper as in the Anglo-Indian papers. We do not hold that bomb-throwing is not a criminal act and is not reprehensible. We condemn it. But in condemning it we say that we must also condemn the repressive measures of Government. I also explain that it is a power which can be created without requiring much preparation. There are certain powers which can be created by means of a physical act. This is nothing of the kind; it is something like a spell and it deserves to be condemned; but in order to repress it and get rid of it, certain reforms are necessary in the administration."[5]

The basic components of Tilak's political ideology that shaped his attitude to bureaucracy and administration were nationalism, democracy and welfarism. In a sense, his ardent nationalism was also derived from his overweening democratic faith. He strongly believed that the Government of this country must be responsible to its people and not to another country and its rulers and political institutions. As long as the policy-makers and decision-makers at the highest level were mostly alien in origin and owed their loyalty to the seat of sovereign power in another country, the principle of responsibility and accountability of the country's government and administration to its own people would not be realized. Aberrations of the nationalistic ideology were also noticeable in Tilak's emphasis on Indian administrative personnel irrespective of their quality and efficiency and attachment to traditional administrative mores and structures. Tilak held that India had to be a welfare state if the democratic professions of British Government in India were genuine. He emphasized that apart from sponsoring development in the sectors of agriculture, industry, crafts, education, health and medicine, social welfare, etc., the state must advance the good of the agriculturists, artisans and craftsmen in rural and urban areas, the factory workers and the government employees in the civil service as well as public utilities like the railways, post and telegraph etc.[6]

But for all these development a proper and supporting bureaucracy was needed and he lamented that the supporting spirit towards the Indian people was absent in that time as far as the bureaucracy was concerned. This is why, Tilak was a bitter critic of bureaucracy. He said in his speech, "It was, as a newspaper editor, my duty to place my views before the Government in a different light from that in which the Anglo-Indian papers thought it fit to do.

Gentlement, here I must say one thing. Although I speak of the Anglo-Indian community, it is not a matter between Anglo-Indians and Indians. Political parties take the form of rival interests between communities in India. But that is not always the case; and in my controversy instead of Anglo-Indian community and Native community, we should say the pro-bureaucracy and anti-bureaucracy party; or if you do not want to use the word 'anti-bureaucracy', let us say the pro-Congress party. These are two parties, if properly defined. The object being to place both sides before the Government." He put stress on his view that he was not against British race but bureaucracy : "I use the word pro-bureaucrat and pro-Congress deliberately in order to show that their interests are not racial interests. It is a mistake to suppose that the controversy arose out of any racial differences."[7] According to him, there was a real opposition of interests, such opposition as was found in England between the Conservatives and Liberals. The opinion of Tilak was that the newspapers were duty bound to convey the merits and demerits of bureaucracy to the Government and if a newspaper could not follow this duty, then it means that the paper failed to perform its duty.

Tilak was an advocate of the freedom of press and we all know that Britain was famous as a nation having respect for the freedom of press. Therefore, Tilak wanted such type of freedom for Indian press also as it was given to the British press, because India was governed by Britain. He said, "We have a right to complain if India is to be governed in a completely arbitrary manner. But India is governed by a nation having respect for the liberty and the freedom of the Press, which sacrificed some of its best men for it. Although the bureaucracy here may be inconvenienced by the principle, it is your duty, gentlemen, to stand between us of the Press and those people and protect us."[8] He challenged the jury to protect the right of the Indian press and people from that of bureaucracy. He said, "You are the guardians of our liberties. I say we want local self-government, local

Home-rule, whatever you may call it. Government at once says, 'there they are; they are discontented and they want a share in the Government. They are acting disrespectfully.' Is it not derogatory to our self-respect and prestige? And if the matter is to be considered like this and the law of sedition is to be considered so rigidly as this, in every case the accused will be found guilty. We had better not have trials at all;" because according to Tilak it was in the hands of Government to send a man to the Andamans without trial. His opinion was that it was not sedition to ask for a share in the power of Government and to complain to Government. It was not seditious to advocate the reformation of the administration or to find fault in it.[9]

Tilak wanted to obtain a large share in the administration of India. He said, "Our remote ideal is a confederacy of the Indian provinces, possessing colonial self-government, with all Imperial questions set apart for the Central Government in England. Perhaps our Home Rule would take the form of provincial councils of fifty or sixty members, nominated or indirectly elected at first, but elected by popular vote as education became more general." But he said that this kind of ideal was far ahead at that time, and perhaps it would come in practice after generations. Therefore, he said, "What we aim at doing now is to bring pressure on the bureaucracy to make it feel that all is not well. Of late the attitude of our British officials has greatly changed for the worse. They no longer speak of educating us up to freedom, as the great Englishmen like Elphinstone did in the past. They appear to agree with the 'Times' that our education in subjects like English history must be checked, because it is dangerous for 'natives' to learn anything about freedom." He said that the Statesmen seemed to take the old Roman Empire as their ideal, and even in that they followed the modern school of Oxford historians who traced the fall of the Empire to the concession of citizenship to the provinces. He compared the Indian bureaucracy with that of Russian bureaucracy and said that though it was a worst bureaucracy but not more than the bureaucracy in India because "... even that bureaucracy does, according to its lights, seek to maintain the honour and prosperity of Russia, because Russia is its own country. Our bureaucracy administers a country not its own for the sake of a country a away, entirely different in character and interests. Our bureaucracy is despotic, alien and absentee."[10]

The main fire of his withering criticism Tilak directed at the rule of the 'autocratic, unrestricted and irresponsible English bureaucracy in India', the 'irresponsible and uncontrolled way or the English Officers in India', the 'English official class'. He exposed the falsity of the British ruling Liberal party which pursued in India, policy of bloody repressions against the patriots. Tilak wrote : "The fact that fiends of repression should swarm everywhere while the Liberal party is in power and while a philosopher and an expounder of the principles of liberalism like Morley is holding the rein of administration, will make it evident to our readers how the rulers themselves had abjured their ideals." What does this policy of repression mean? Tilak asked and answered himself that repression pursued a definite aim and that was to stop the future progress of those causes which had given birth to the nation in India, which had developed the nation and which had created the national fire for the rise of nation. He pointed out that "to drag those causes backwards by pulling them by the leg is called retrograde or repressive policy." He stressed that, "Liberty of speech and liberty of the Press give birth to a nation and nourish it. Seeing that this had begun to turn India into a nation, the Bureaucracy had for many days entertained the desire to smash both of them; and they have fulfilled their strong desire by taking advantage of the bomb in Bengal."[11]

Tilak stigmatised the repressive policy of the bureaucracy as a policy of retrogrades and reactionaries. He denounced this policy as one based on the maxim that the rulers can practise whatever oppression they like, deport anyone they choose without trial, partition any province, stop any meeting at their will, prosecute anyone they like for sedition and send him to jail, while the people must silently endure all these things and not allow their indignation, exasperation or vehemence to go beyond certain bound. Tilak pointed out that the country was sustaining tremendous losses from the political, industrial, moral and material point of view, owing to the entire administration of India being carried on solely under the guidance of the English official class and in utter disregard of public opinion. Tilak wrote that "the rule of the autocratic, unrestricted and irresponsible English bureaucracy in India is becoming more and more unbearable tothe people."[12] Referring to the tremendous loss India sustained from being administrated by "English bureaucrats inebriated with the isolence of authority" Tilak stressed that "in order to prevent this loss the power inthe hands of the English bureaucracy must by degrees be transferred to our hands; there is no other alternative", the rule of authority "should come into the hands of the people."[13] Tilak thought that these were the repressive methods of bureaucracy which forced the people to become revolutionary. Therefore he urged the Government that "instead of leaving to the people the work of bringing about revolution, "it should of its own accord "begin to effect proper reforms inthe system of administration; this will prove more beneficial both to the people and the Government."[14] Tilak wanted to bring pressure on bureaucaracy for the effective representation in administration for Indians, and for this purpose he wrote several articles in his newspapers. These articles were against the bureaucarcy, because he thought that"... if the times are times of unrest, it becomes the duty of a newspaper man to impress upon Government the cause of that unrest. It is a very hard duty — a very thankless duty and sometimes a very risky duty. I understand it very well, but it has to be done. If the newspaper is to go on for the benefit of the people and the interest of the Government, you cannot allow any other consideration to interfere with your duty."[15] He said that they had not started those papers to earn money only.

They had started them to discuss current topics and public questions and for creating public opinion in the country. He urged the Government to help them is performing their duty. He said that before declaring an article seditious or objectionable, the Government had to examine the motive of the publication and the other facts, which influenced the writer. If his motive was good, if he was trying to secure constitutional rights of the people in a fair way and a persevering manner, he was entitled to express his views fully and fearlessly, because it would be beneficial for the progress of the country. Tilak said that 'these are the English traditions' and the Indians admired them, but, so long as the Indians admired them "you are pleased, but as soon as we begin to limitate them you call it seditious."[16] This was a wrong tradition. He said that the bureaucracy had long enjoyed absolute arbitrary powers, and the Indians were fighting against it. Therefore, it was a great struggle between the bureaucracy and the people and the Government had support of the people. He cited the example of the Cox's Criminal Law, page 51, charge of Lord Fitizgerald in the case Rex Vs Sullivan, in his famous trial an dasked to judge the motives of a man and said that when a power is arbitrarily exercised it must be restricted.[17] He said : "Journalists have perfect freedom to discuss measures of Government, to disapprove of them and to use forcible language, if necessary, and to do everything which is legitimately honest in bringing before the public and the Government the fact that their measures or actions are disapproved by a section of the public or by a particular speaker or by a particular journalist. He is entitled to urge every reason that he can in forcibled language to show his views with regard tothe administrative or executive acts of Government."[18]

Tilak could not understand why the Indian press had the same privilege in this country as the English press enjoyed at home. According to him, "It is a very important question. It is the same question which was fought out by Erskine in the case of Dean of St. Asaph. It is the question that ws fought out in England as long ago as 1792. English people now enjoy the liberty of the Press which they demanded and got in the 18th century." This was the same case in the opinion of Tilak and all that he wanted from the jury was a patient hearing. He said, "You are proud of your traditions. You have got the liberty of the Press after a long struggle and I believe that you attach more importance to that then even we do here. I can trace a great struggle between the people on the one hand and a mighty Bureaucracy on the other. And I ask you to help us not me personally but the whole of India in our endeavours to obtain share in Government of this country." He asked for justice because this was a critical question. This was not only connected with the transportation of Tilak but with the future also, because the future generation would judge the verdict, whether it was wrong or right; and according to Tilak, "The verdict is likely to be a memorable one in the history of the struggle for the freedom of the Indian Press."[19]

Time had proved how corredt Tilak was in regard to his views on freedom of the press. The verdict not only became a momorable one in the history of the struggle for the freedom of press, but also in the histroy of the struggle for the Indian freedom. Nowadays we all remember it as a bitter and partial verdict, which was intentionally brought in existence for Tilak, because he was a most powerful Indian leader of that time and the British government wanted to send him far away from the country. Tilak's arguments against the repressive methods of bureaucracy and his demand for share in the administration for Indian people, did upset the British government and the bureaucracy and they began to look at him as an alarm of danger for the British regime.

The verdict can be criticized on another basis also. In 1942 Gandhi also had to face a trial under the same section of the Indian Penal Code, but he was not ransported to Mandalay. He still remained imprisoned in India. This was a clear example of the partial justice under the British regime.

If the offence took place under the same section of law, how could the judgement diffrer?

Tilak was also correct in saying that the bureaucracy was not Government and there was a difference between the bureaucracy and the Government. This difference was not in existence in the British regime only but it remains upto now also and perhaps it will remain for ever. We can identify bureaucracy as a working machine of the Government, because it is bureaucracy which is responsible for the implementation of the decisions of the Government. Here is an example to strengthen this argument:

There was a not on the table of a chief minister on the occasion of the meeting of N.D.C. at Vigyan Bhawan, Delhi, where the Fifth Five Year Plan was being discussed. A story written in that note was that there was a rat who was very much terrified by a cat. This is why the rat went to the wise creature owl, for the advice for which he could get rid of the problem. The owl advised him to become a cat. The rat became very happy and went home, but he did not understand how he could become a cat. Therefore, again he went to the owl the next day. The owl became angry and said that his duty was only concerned with the policy-making. This depends on the rat as to how he will implement it.[20]

It becomes very clear from this example that this is totally the responsibility of bureaucracy to obey the decisions of the Government. Here the rat is a symbol of bureaucracy and the owl is a symbol of the Government. It depends on bureaucracy whether it implements the decisions of the Government in perfect manner or not. The people of the country are not connected with the Government directly, but with the bureaucracy. The right and wrong work of bureaucracy affects the people directly. We can say that bureaucracy is a chain that links the people and the Government. If the bureaucracy will be able and perfect, the people will be benefited and the country would also become prosperous and progressive, but if the bureaucracy runs in an arbitrary manner. the position will be the reverse and in the reverse position it is natural that a struggle will start between the bureaucracy and the people. Therefore, Tilak was quite correct in saying that bureaucracy was not the Government and the criticism of bureaucracy is not the criticism of the Government.

Footnotes

1. Inamdar, *op, cit.,* p. 57.
2. Govt. of India, Publication Division (Publisher), *Trial of Tilak,* p. 179.
3. *Ibid.,* p. 180.
4. *Ibid.*
5. *Ibid.*
6. Inamdar, *op. cit.,* p. 56.
7. Varma, *op. cit.,* p. 280.
8. Trial of Tilak, *op. cit.,* p. 116.
9. *Ibid.*
10. H.W. Nevinson, *The New Spirit of India,* London, Herper and Brothers, 1908, p. 72.
11. I.M. Reinsner and N.M. Goldberg (eds.), *Tilak and the Struggle for Idnian Freedom,* New Delhi, People's Publishing House, 1966, p. 555.
12. *Ibid.,* p. 556.
13. *Ibid.,* p. 558.
14. *Ibid.,* p. 562.
15. Varma, *op. cit.,* p. 280.
16. Trial of Tilak, *op. cit.,* p. 115.
17. *Ibid.,* p. 116.
18. Varma, *op. cit.,* p. 291.
19. Trial of Tilak, *op. cit.,* p. 118.
20. *The Statesman,* 22nd Jan. 1973.

6 Political Resources and Means

Tilak twinned the concept of nationalism with 'Swaraj'. According to him, "It does not require high interllectual gifts to understand the meaning of Swaraj. It is a simple Sanskrit word, meaning nothing more or less than the power to rule our homes, and hence it is called in short Home Rule. It is your birthright to govern your own house or home, nobody else can claim to do it."[1] But for attainment of Swaraj, Tilak believed only in constitutional means. He spoke at Yeotmal: "Whatever that be, one thing is certain, that the work before us is not easy. Tremendous sacrifices will be necessary: nay, we shall have todie for it; there are two ways of dying, one constitutional and other unconstitutional. As our fight is going to be constitutional and legal, our death also must, as of necessity, be constitutional and legal, our death also must, as of necessity, be constitutional and legal. We have not to use any violence. Nay, we condemn the unconstitutional way of doing. As our fight must be constitutional it must be courageous also. We ought to tell Government courageously and without the least fear what we want. Let the Government know that the whole nation wants Home Rule. Let there be no shirking, or wavering or shaking."[2] Thus, for attainment of 'Swaraj' through constitutional means, Tilak adopted some technics as :

Swadeshi Boycott and Passive Resistance

The partition of Bengal was the immediate cause of the Swadeshi movement. An agitation against it was carried on under the leadership of Tilak, Pal, Aurobindo and Surendranath Benerjea. The anti-partition movement in India has to be analysed in the light of the growing intensification of the Asiatic political consiousness manifested by the Boxer movement of China, the victories of Japan over Russia and the growth of national movements in Persia and Turkey. Lokamanya was a student of international politics. As early as 1895, commenting on the Sino-Japanese War of 1894-95 he had written in the Kesari that the condition of Japan was like a representative of the revolution proceeding in Asia. He had predicted that the defeat of China would lead to a patriotic awakening of that big country. In several articles in the Kesari, Tilak acknowledged the great inspiration received by the Asiatic youth from the political triumphs of Japan over Russia. Japan's signal ascendancy was a standing refutation of the myth of Asiatic inferiority. Some inspiration to Indian youth was also provided by the boycott campaign of the Chinese against the exclusivist orientation of immigration policy of the United States.[3]

On October 16, 1905, the partition resolution was put into operation and the day was observed as a day of mourning in Bengal. Many people fasted on that day all business transactions were stopped, foreign cloth was burnt and in temples vows of Swedeshi began to be taken.[4] From 1899 to 1904, Tilak could not get the necessary opportunity to carry on dynamic political agitation, but the anti-partition agitation gave him the much sought opportunity of intensified political action. Lokamanya now emerged and triumphed as an all-India leader. It was the supreme insight of Tilak that turned an agitation for territorial change into an all-India movement for national emancipation. Due to his efforts Bengal and Maharashtra and partly also the Punjab were united by the indissoluble bond of common political affiliations. The personality and action of leaders like Tilak,

Lala Lajpat Rai, Bipin Chandra Pal, and Aurobindo Ghose transformed the anti-partition movement into a crusade for the regeneration of a fallen nation.[5]

Tilak tried to transmute the anti-partition agitation into a movement for the Swaraj of the country. 'Swadeshi', Boycott and 'Passive resistance' were the various technics of the movement of 'Swaraj'. This movement of 'Swaraj' and 'Swadeshi' was to supplement the work of Congress. The Congress had confined itself to the educated classes; the Swadeshi movement attempted to bring not only the lower middle classes but also the masses into some sort of political and economic action. Thus, Tilak and the other lieutenants of his in Bengal and Maharashtra were trying to transform the prevailing concept of politics. The Swadeshi-boycott movement was a mighty attempt at vindicating the rights of the people to self-government, and hence, it perfected several technics of political agitation as, mass processions, big public meetings, strikes, picketings etc., which have been followed by the later Indian leaders intheir political movements.[6] The Swadeshi-boycott movement was an organized attempt for the assertion of the great democratic principle, that the predominant political opinion of the inhabitants of a country must not be transgressed by the rulers. This movement has to be understood from the general sociological standpoint of the genesis and growth of modern Indian nationalism, since the seventies and eighties of the last century. Indian capitalism was rising and the new bourgeoisie of Calcutta and Bombay finanacially helped the movement of Swadeshi because it made a passionate propaganda for things made in India. The growth of natioalism in India, however, was not a mere consequence of the rise of capitalism. Nationalism, in India, manifested itself as a profoundly spiritual and religious phenomenon.[7]

Tilak had lost faith in the cult of appeals. His solution of the problem was intensification of the nationalist agitation. In Maharashtra the Swadeshi movement had started much earlier. Tilak felt that only Swadeshi and boycott would force the bureaucracy to grant conscessions. On the 15th of August (1905) Tilak wrote an article captioned "The Hour of Destiny. Sanskrit quotation at the commencement : "A filament of a lotus cannot arrest an elephant fresh in the rut", implied that no repression would thwart the powerful Swadeshi movement that had been started. He commended the Town Hall resolution and said that "the mouth is opened only by shinthing the nose, and the Government will not stop its arrogance unless we do something that severely affects it... It is clear now that mighty speeches lead us nowhere; not words, but action is wanted — determined action... A day has come in the progress of public opinion in India, when our leaders have either to move with a will and determination and achieve their objective or rot in the poisonous atmosphere."[8]

Tilak attached greater importanc eto boycott as a means of exercising pressure on Britain to compel them to grant Indians legitimate rights. According to him, "To rebel against government illegally is an offence, but a boycott is not".[9]

Tilak felt that the Congress should pursue a bolder line of action than before. He said : "The British rule in India is for the benefit of Englishmen and our rulers, policy has been to give some rights to Indians if their own interests are not affected... Our opinion is that we should not let our miseries before our rulers and make requests, because such requests are futile. The Indian National Congress should carefully think over all these matters and decide whether time has or has not come for making a change in their policy... It is no use simply crying for rights or begging for them; we must insist upon our rights and do all that we can."[10] "It is true", he said, "that people have not yet developed adequate strength to destroy British rule and to establish Swaraj; but it is possible to make administration deplorably difficult and to create conditions impossible for the British bureaucracy, by fighting for our rights with determination and tenacity and by boycott and strikes. It has been well said that freedom's struggle once begun, is never lost, but ever won."[11]

Speaking about constitutional agitation, he said that the terms do not apply to India but only such countries where the constitution provides for popular control over the government :

> "There is no such constitution in India. The government in India is irresponsible and non-constitutional. Constituted authorities in India are irresponsible and we have to take our rights from them. The legality of our action is decided by this government. Our actions may be illegal according to their point of view but we should not worry whether our agitation is legal or illegal. We must see whether justice, morality and historical tradition are in our favour or not, and if our actions are correct according to these standards we should not care as to whether they come within the law or not, because, the power of making laws is in the hands of foreigners. Of course, it is true that the infringement of the law is oppressive, it should be resisted only suffering such punishment, there is no other way. This is bound to happen when the law and morality are in conflict with each other."[12]

The growth of Swadeshi movement was intolerable for the bureaucracy and it was determined to suppress the movement. The Barisal Conference (April 1906) showed the coercive technics of the Government in utter ruthlessness. The climax of police oppression was revealed at the Conference, when the police assaulted the delegates and forcibly disparsed the meeting. Tilak was indignant at this act of police repression and excess. He wrote a series of articles in Kesari denouncing the policy and action of the Government. On the 17th April, 1906, he expressed deep remorse and grief at the humiliation meted out to Surendranath. He condemned the Government circular which banned the uttering of the slogan of 'Bande Mataram' on public streets. On May 8, 1906, he began a critical comment on the Barisal incident with a Sanskrit Quotation "त्वं चेन्नीचपधेन गच्छसि पयः कस्त्वां निरोद्धुं क्षमः।" He warned the Government against taking recourse to the technics of the Czarist autocracy and hoped that the liberal tradition would be continued. In another article in the Kesari entitled "The Government and the Barisal Incident", dated the 15th May, 1906, he welcomed the move of Bengal leaders who had agitated for obtaining the right to sing the slogan of 'Bande Mataram.'[13]

Tilak's comment on the incident was; "Repression is repression, whether legal or illegal. If it is a legal repression, it must be resisted peacefully with determination to suffer the penalty. If it is illegal, then it must be illegally met... It is the people's right to decide whether the action of Government is proper or oppressive."[14]

Tilak felt that Swadeshi and boycott were the technics and instruments for the realization of Swaraj. By honest Swadeshism, the Government meant non-political Swadeshi. In other words, honest Swadeshism was purely economic Swadeshism without political orientation. Such an economic Swadeshism was possible only in a free and industrialized country. It is true that when the Swadeshi movement had started in the Bombay Presidency in the last century it was economic in character. But as the political situation of India was very critical, Tilak and Pal felt that Swadeshism should be used as a pressure upon the alien and unrepentant bureaucracy. The official circle could only tolerate a policy of Swadeshism within the limits of free trade. But Tilak and Pal were committed to the policy of protection for an economically weak and backward country like India. The boycott of foreign goods and especially British goods could be used as a lever to support the infant home industries and thus to promote economic development.[15]

Tilak's preaching of passive resistance was not an idea which came to him on the impulse of the moment. He had given careful thought to it and had discussed the subject on several occasions in Kesari.[16] The Benaras Congress marked an important stage inthe political career of Tilak, for with his declaration of the principles of passive resistance, he burnt his boats on the burning ghats of the sacred city of Benares. Thinkers and philosophers such as Thorow in America and Tolstoy in Russia had put forward the abstract theory of passive resistance, but no one before Tilak had dressed it in everyday clothes and given it to the people to put into practice. After the Benaras Congress Tilak's fight for India's independence was threefold, for it was carried on three fronts. On the first front he was working to rouse the people to fight for the country's freedom; on the second front he was exposing the weak and timid policies of the moderate leaders; and on the third front he was opposing the repressive measures of the Government, which became more savage as the people's demand for self-government grew. It can be said that in the years between 1905 and 1908. Tilak founded "The People of India". It was during this period that for the first time a definite form was given to the idea of Indian nationalism.[17]

The Benaras Congress passed the important resolution on economic enquiry and land renenue policy, which had been moved by Tilak. He delivered a lecture at the time of moving the resolution, in which he remarks : "We have all heard of the Swadeshi movement going on all over the country. Anglo-Indian officials are claiming that they are Swadeshi in this land. So there are others, especially famine and plague; they are claiming that they are Swadeshis. They want to make India their home;... and we want to boycott them."[18]

In the above remarks, we find an indirect meaning of Tilak's idea also, that like famine and plague, he wanted to boycott the Anglo-Indianofficials also. Tilak sent his followers (after Benaras Congress) home to think over his programme of passive resistance and report to him the next year in Calcutta.[19]

The Calcutta Congress passed the important resolution on self-government. Swadeshi and boycott in this famous historic session. Lala Lajpat Rai points out that these resolutions could be carried through only due to the initiative, political vigour and firm determination of Lokamanya who was in Calcutta with the entire staff of his political lieutenants. According to Tilak, "The Twenty-second Indian National Congress had given us a new start... It is satisfactory that the managers or the directors of the Congress, rather the retiring boards of directors have accepted this ideal." His idea was that "Swadeshi is the first step, boycott is the means and Swaraj is the end."[20]

On January 2, 1907, Tilak delivered a historic speech on "Tenets of the New Party", in which he defined self-government as a goal of the New Party: "The point is to have the entire control in our hands. I want to have the key of my house... Self-government is our goal; we want a control over our administrative machinery. We do not want to become clerks." Tilak did not cherish the spirit of uncompromising fanaticism and irreconcilable intransigence in politics. He would take what he would get and then struggle for the remainder. This was the essence of the political methodology. Hence, the dominant ideology of the New Party was the concept of self-help understood in terms of Swadeshi and boycott. Boycott was to be interpreted not merely in the passive and static sense of economic boycott but was regarded as the dynamic technic of passive resistance. Tilak said : "Are you prepared in this way to fight if your demand is refused? If you are, be sure you will not be refused; but if you are not, nothing can be more certain than that your demand will be refused, and perhaps for ever. We are not armed and there is no necessity for arms either. We have a stronger weapon, a political weapon in boycott."[21]

Tilak appealed to the students to make success of the Swadeshi movement. The moderate leaders felt that the students should confine themselves to the academic world. Gokhale's idea was that students should take some part in the educational growth of the people by trying to disseminate education to fellow-countrymen in vacations. Tilak argued that this ideal was suited for normal peaceful times but when the country was engaged in a furious struggle with the bureaucracy, students should do something to help the national movement. Tilak seriously condemned the attitude of Principal Pranjpye who had imposed a fine of ten rupees on Savarkar, then a student of Fergusson College, for breach of discipline. On 27th November and 4th December, 1906, Tilak wrote two articles in the Kesari, on the problem of the role of students in the national movements. He acknowledged that the existing institutions were imparting education in Bacon, Milton and Shakespeare, but it was also essential to train the students in patriotic sentiments and national activities. Tilak said that if students would not participate in political action because of the "discipline" of the institutions, if in the prime of life there was the fear of losing Government service to prevent political activities and if during old age the pension rules acted as a sword of Damocles, then there would be no freedom throughout life and the whole generation would be enervated and this tradition of national enervation would pass to succeeding generations leading to national collapse. Tilak felt that if teachers deliberately stood against the rights of students to get an independent nationally oriented education, they should be disobeyed. He quoted the statement of Mahabharat — "रोद्रः क्षत्रियधोडेयं गुरूणा यदयुध्यत" – to support this view.[22]

Tilak advised the agriculturists also to take the vow of Swadeshi. According to Tilak Swadeshi movement was not sponsored by the aristocracy. It was meant for the labourers because they got wages from the native mills. As an economic realist, he told the workers that the Swadeshi movement aimed at providing work for the labouring population. Therefore, we see that Tilak wanted participation of all kinds of people in the Swadeshi movement. His idea was : "Swadeshism is a large term which includes politics and to be a true Swadeshi, one must look on all lines — whether political or industrial or economical which converge our people towards the status of civilized nation."[23]

Talking about passive resistance, he said : "Passive resistance was the means to an end but was not the goal in itself. Passive resistance meant that they had to balance the advantages and disadvantages arising from obeying a particular order and not obeying it. It was a determination to achieve their goal at any sacrifices."[24] It was Tilak's policy of passive resistance, which under the inspiring leadership and guidance of Mahatma Gandhi assumed gigantic proportions after 1920 and which India practised for a quarter of a century, under different labels and with varying success. First it was called Non-co-operation, in 1930-31. Civil disobedience and in 1942 it became known as Satyagraha. Whatever the name given to Gandhi's movement, the basic principles enunciated by Tilak at Benaras — namely, withholding the people's willing co-operation from the Government — remained unchanged."[25]

It is true that Mahatma Gandhi made Tilak's principles more attractive and acceptable to the masses by giving them a spiritual interpretation; it is also true that, presented as a spiritual programme, the Civil disobedience practised under Gandhi's leadership gained vastly in prestige as a political weapon and had a greater effect. Yet the fact remains that it was the vision and courage of Tilak which conceived the enormous possibilities of passive resistance as a political weapon — perhaps the only weapon of the people completely disarmed and demoralised by a long period of slavery which they could use against an alien government."[26]

Three Instrument

B.R. Keldar says that Tilak's politics had no precedent on any model to be followed. Tilak created his own tools and technics of political awakening. For this purpose Tilak shaped three instruments. First was the press, second was the public opinion (Lokmat) and the third was the radicalisation of Indian National Congress. The political objective of fashioning all these instruments was togive a democratic and mass orientation to the political awakening in India.[27]

Press

Tilak held the view that press had a right to criticise the bureaucracy. In fact, it was the duty of the newspapers to place before the Government the grievances of the people. Tilak used to ask, "We have not started the papers for winning the favour of the Government. We shall not be sorry for its displeasure, because of our criticism of its policy. Nor will we hesitate to suffer the consequences of that displeasure. If the repressive policy of the Government is not to be protested against and if we are not to tell the people that the folly of the administration will cause them suffering, and that all such acts of the Government will not be in the interests of the Government itself, why then have any paper at all?"[28]

He said that "Our views and the way in which they are expressed may sound harsh; but that is so because of the way of our thinking; when the heart burns under protest against disgusting wrongs and gross injustice, that fire will naturally be reflected in the writings and expressions of the writer." Kesari was the first instrument which Tilak headed. He was one of the promoters of Kesari and, therefore, its policy-maker. In their first announcement about the publication in January 1881, the promoters said that Kesari would speak the truth as they saw. The announcement said, "There is no doubt that hypocrisy and sycophancy is on the rise since the advent of the imperial rule. Every honest man will accept that this is an unbecoming development which is harming the nation's interest. You can take it that the articles appearing in this paper will be in keeping with its title." This showed that Kesari would be a journal with a different outlook. Tilak wished to make Kesari 'the voice of common people'. Later, after twenty years Tilak wrote, "In the pre-Kesari era, newspapers mostly carried articles to let the rulers know their views to the educated classes. The times have changed. We do not have only the rulers in mind. We tackle broader issues like present system of Government, its weaknesses and how these can be set right. Our primary aim is to awaken the people and to create conditions for the use of this organised power "(Kesari, 11Feb., 1902). Tilak's political philosophy started taking shape through the columns of Kesari from 1888 when he took over its editorship.[29]

Public Opinion

The second instrument which Tilak forged was the public opinion (Lokmat). It was the keystone of the democratic politics of Tilak. In a controversy over the 'brute force', in 1895, Tilak told Gokhale that "for us public opinion is of foremost importance" (Adya-daivat). This was not an argument put forward as a retort to an opponent in a political controversy, but a statement of basic faith of Tilak in the supremacy of the public opinion. He always used the pressure of volatile public opinion against certain oppressive laws, objectionable bills circulated by the Government and redressal of grievances during famine.[30]

Indian National Congress

The third instrument which Tilak evolved was the Indian National Congress. His views was that Congress was an organisation of the people and that the voice of the people ought to predominate. He, therefore, wanted to give a mass base to the Congress and a democratic direction to its functioning.[31]

Was Tilak a Revolutionary?

Many of the critics of Tilak regard him as a revolutionary. Chirol wrote in his book 'India' : "Tilak had been the first to create the atmosphere which breeds murders." John S. Hoyland says that Tilak had been "conquetting with doctrines of physical force". Branson, the Advocate-General who conducted the prosecution case against Tilak, in 1908, said that Tilak's articles contained "a covert threat of mutiny" and in substance he was preaching "Swarajya or bombs". It is true that Tilak did not rule out the possibility of revolution as a means of achieving independence, and it is also true that he was in touch with some of the leading revolutionaries of those days, like Shyamji Krishnaverma, whom he compared with Hyndman, in an article of Kesari, and Savarkar family and others; but it is also true that there is no concrete and positive evidence to prove that he himself was a terrorist or an anarchist revolutionary. The critics also referred the book 'Mazzini', written by V.D. Savarkar, which was dedicated to Lokamanya Tilak as well as S.M. Paranjpye.[32] But this only shows the high gratitude of Savarkar towards Tilak. Tilak knew Savarkar well and besides this Savarkar was highly inspired by Tilak and so he dedicated his book to Lokamanya. It does not give the evidence that Tilak was also a revolutionary like Savarkar.

Some critics called Tilak revolutionary because he was behind the planning to open an arms factory in Nepal, but this plan could not be fulfilled. A similar attempt was made by Vasukaka Joshi on the north-western front, but the plan however did not materialize.[33] But these incidents only show that Lokamanya wanted to open an arms factory in Nepal or in Afghanistan, but it does not indicate clearly that he had plans of creating an armed revolution against British regime. Acharya Javedkar said in a personal interview : "Tilak believed in the inherent right of India to attain political freedom even by a violent revolution."[34] He also said that "Tilak approved of the revolutionary activities of a preparatory nature for he visualized that although the peaceful struggle may lead the country to the very precincts of Swarajya, at the last moment this method may not be sufficient and the violent revolutionaries would be required to play some part."[35]

P.S. Khankhoje in a series of articles contributed to the Kesari in August 1953 and February 1954, has tried to interpret Lokamanya as a teacher and preceptor of the revolutionary youth of the country. It is true that these letters refer to a phase of Tilak's personality which had not been well-known so far. But still they do not give any concrete and positive evidence to prove that Lokamanya himself was a violent terrorist or an anarchist revolutionary.[36] V.M. Bhatt of Poona holds that till 1908 Tilak closely associated with revolutionists and encouraged them. He says that Tilak did not refer to revolutionary actions and policies in his speeches and writings but only disclosed them to persons in his close confidence like Khadilkar and Vasukaka Joshi. It is true that Tilak never accepted the absolute form of non-violence as upheld by the pacifists and Leo Tolstoy, but he felt that the situation in the country was not suitable for the revolutionary activity. Once he said : "From begging to open rebellion choose anything according to your ability and do it, but remember —"स्वधर्मे निधन श्रेयः, परधर्मो भयावहः ।"[37]

Tilak did not approve of the idea of wasting the cream of Indian youth in an effort which was not at all likely to bear fruit. Tilak unlike Gandhi did not look upon non-violence as a creed or a philosophy. But as a practical statesman he knew that it was not worthwhile taking to illegal methods, for it would be playing into the hands of the British. Tilak always advocated the need for manifold means — साधनानामनेवता — for getting Swaraj. To him the constitutional efforts of the moderates and the direct action of revolutionaries — all these appeared to be necessary in fighting the British. He insisted that means must be appropriate to the circumstances and the times. Though he criticised the moderates he always acknowledged that at a particular stage in Indian politics, petitions and requests did serve an important purpose. On the other hand he tried to restrain the young radicals because he thought that insurrectionary methods were inopportune. His advice to young revolutionaries was "Keep your powder dry".[38]

In his article of Kesari in 1908, Tilak underlined his appraisal by citing the unpreparedness of the masses, pointing out that the ideas of revolution had not yet gripped the minds of the people and so far were harboured only by a few Indians holding politically advanced views.[39] Tilak insistently cited not only the example of the English revolution of 1642. In his articles of that period he repeatedly alluded to the Russian revolution, and the revolutions in France and Germany. But, Tilak held that the time of revolution had not yet arrived, that there were yet no conditions for violent revolutionary struggle to immediately overthrow the colonial regime. Tilak was not like Ajit Singh, who called the people to immediate rebellion, mainly believing that Indians need but desire it and the colonial regime would be swept away. The native confidence of such political leaders was based on simple artihmetic; there were over 300,000,000 Indians and but a handful of British, a mere 150,000 sacrificing themselves in a spirit of dedication Indians certainly could destroy the British one by one, and there would be none left in India. But tthey underestimated the strength of the enemy and his social mainstay in India. At the same time their call to immediately exterminate the British and their belief that was necessary to accomplish it, was a heroic self-sacrifice of the Indians.[40] Tilak held that even such ineffective means of struggle as individual terror was better than passivity and slavish submission to the British. But he was aware that individual terror was not the proper means to liberate India, for any killed bureaucrat would be replaced by others and the British administration would not be undermined.[41] Tilak felt that the revolutionaries were not treading the correct path, but he admired their courage and not take any action or utter any word which would discourage them, but this is also true that he never encouraged those persons. The reminiscences of some people in Maharashtra who were then engaged in revolutionary work and of some whose minds were working in that direction are very significant in this respect.

Shri Gangadharrao Deshpande, the eminent leader of Belgaum and a disciple of Tilak, has also writtten the following reminiscences : "Lokamanaya came to Belgaum for the Ganapati festival in 1906 for tthe first time. After the procession, Lokamanya said to me privately, "I have only recently returned from Nasik. There also I saw such young men and I met some of them. Their enthusiasm and ambition are unique. But they are rather foolish. You look after your young men, for such folly ruins the work." At this time there was a group revolutionaries who had formed an organisation at Nasik called Abhinav Bharat under the leadership of Savarkar brothers. A member of this association has written the following accounts of his talks with Tilak. He wrote, "We met Lokamanya and asked him to join our organisation and cited the instance of some other country that had gained independence by the same method. Lokamanaya said, 'It is true that our condition and the condition of that country was similar. But in our country there is no unrest among the masses as it existed there. Otherwise we would also have left the constitutional ways and followed their methods. Still many people believe that the English have come here to benefit us. The duty of the leaders at present is first to remove this notion and to explain to the people that the English have come to drain and impoverish India. If we try to risk a rebellion today, people would not be ready to join it. Mangoes are not gathered before they ripe, and remember, if you make haste the mango is spoilt." Tilak thus regarded it his responsibility to prevent any hasty sentimental action. He was favourable for a preparation for revolution, but he did not favour any immediate action. Tilak's conception of preparing for an eventful full-fledged revolution in India was far wider than that of the underground workers. His own political activities were directed to the creation of two thought currents and sentiments among the masses. In the first place, he wanted to promote the spirit of nationalism which would enable people to transcend the limits of caste and religion and stand as one unit against the foreign domination. Secondly, he was creating among the masses a consciousness of their political rights and was teaching them the new and modern methods of criticising and peacefully fighting against the political injustice.[42]

Tilak called for broadening of the mass struggle against British colonial rule in India, pointing out that the aim of the struggle was a revolution, but which type of revolution, about this he said: "It is true that what we seek may seem like a revolution. It is a revolution in the sense that it means a complete change in the theory of the Government of India as now put forward by the bureaucracy. It is true that this revolution must be a bloodless revolution, but it would be a folly to suppose that if there is to be no shedding of blood, there are also to be no sufferings to be undergone by the people. These sufferings must be great, you can win nothing unless you are prepared to suffer."[43] Therefore, we see that though Tilak did not hate the revolutionaries, but he himself was nver a supporter of an armed revolt at that time. Some of the great Indian leaders, who had worked with Tilak, also have denied that Tilak was a revolutionary. Bipin Chandra Pal, a colleague of Lokamanya for over a decade, wrote :

> "Tilak never was a revolutionary. His temperament, his superior native intelligence, his very liberal education, his grasp of the actualities of the political situation in his country, all these are absolutely inconsistent with the very idea of any sort of real revolutionary patriotism."[44]

He also remarks that "Chirol evidently drawing his inspiration from some narrow visioned Bombay bureaucrats has completely failed to seize the inner character of this great Brahmin politician." Pal denied that 'he had any real revolutionary aims.' He wrote : "It can't be denied that like many others, especially among the thought leaders of the Nationalist movement in India, he too did want to put in some element of self-confidence and even self-assertiveness in his countrymen; and in so far as they did it, their words misread and their real intentions misunderstood by some people, who simply caught their patriotic enthusiasm without being able to grasp the fundamental psychology or philosophy of national life that really prompted these; and thus turned from steady sober but devoted and lawful workers into violent and hysteric revolutionaries."[45]

Aurobindo, another colleague of Tilak, wrote : "It is equally a mistake to think of Tilak as by nature a revolutionary leader; that is not his character or his political temperament... such a man is no natural revolutionist, but a constitutionalist by temper." C.R. Das also holds that Lokamanaya was not a revolutionary. There was 'no dark plunge of the revolutionary in him'. Das thinks that Tilak was a conservative by instinct, and compromise was the essence of his politics although he never lost signs of the ideal to which his whole being moved.[46]

Conclusion

Tilak wanted to bring Swaraj for India, and was paying full attention for it. He wanted to remove the pressure of three d's : daridrya (poverty), dushkal (famine) and dravyashodha (sucking up the wealth) and it was not possible without Swaraj. But for attainment of Swaraj he was against the moderates' three p's tactics : pleas, prayers and petitions. He called for a mass struggle, because he knew that mothing could be possible without this. The first 25 years of Kesari constantly came across anxious expressions for protection and promotion of the interests of the peasants, workers, artisans, shopkeepers, weavers, Bhils and Katkaris. In an article onfactories he said, "A country may be rich or poor, free or bondage, but its majority population consists of those who live by their bodily labour and unless and until they are happy and contented, their country cannot be regarded as prosperous or progressive."[47]

He wanted a mass struggle represented by all castes and classes of the people for the national movement of India; but he never believed that the terrorist or the military leaders by themselves would ever be able to overthrow the established government in India, unless it was backed by the people with active sympathy and support. Tilak was a practical leader, therefore, he knew that : "Unorganised, disarmed and still disunited, we should not have a chance of shaking the British suzerainty. We may leave all that sort of thinking to distant time. Our object is to obtain eventually a large share in the administration of our own country." Tilak wanted of bring pressure on bureaucracy and for this purpose he adopted some legal means like Swadeshi, Boycott and Passive resistance; for which he said : "Besides Swadeshi movement we work by boycott and passive resistance. Our boycott is voluntary. We do not advocate picketing or compulsory prevention from the purchase of foreign goods. And in passive resistance we shall simply refuse to notice such measures as the Seditious Meeting Act. But we do not care what happens to ourselves. We are devoted absolutely and without reservation to the cause of the Indian people. To imprison even 3,000 or 4,000 of us at the same time would embarrass the bureaucracy."[48]

Thus, it can be said that the Swadeshi movement was a mass movement to bring pressure on bureaucracy. Its character was spiritual, political as well as economical. Gokhale had pointed out that the Swadeshi movement was a patriotic movement for the expansion of production by the rational harnessing of capital, enterprise and skill. It became a movement for the liberation of the spiritual energies of the nation for the sake of the political emancipation of the land. But in its economic roots it was a movement supported by the bourgeoisie for the growth and expansion of early capitalism in India.[49] Therefore, we can say that this was Tilak who showed the path of Swadeshi and passive rsistance, on which his successors like Gandhi walked fastly and smoothly and got the success. But unlike Gandhi, Tilak never discouraged the revolutinaries, though he was never an advocate of illegal actions or armed revolution. He accepted non-violence only on moral grounds.

He did not preach unruliness or illegality but he preached firm determination to reach the goal at any sacrifice. B.C. Pal says about his legal principles : "He was even in the exciting days of the Swadeshi agitation at themost a passive resistor, who set a much narrower limit to his propaganda of passive resistance than what Gandhi openly and admittedly did in South Africa."[50] Tilak made a clear distinction between law and Constitution. He said : "Law and Constitution were not the same. That was proved by History. So long as a particular law was not in conformity with justice and morality, and popular opinion according to the ethics of the 19th and 20th centuries, so long as a particular order was not consistent with all these principles it might be legal, but it was not constitutional."[51]

He wanted people to confine themselves strictly to constitutional means, but in India, the position was different, because here, there was no constitutional document of a fundamental nature to rely upon. Thus, everyone might have his own method provided it was constitutional. Passive resistence was perfectly constitutional, according to Tilak, because it did not preach unruliness or illegality.

Here, we find a fundamental difference between Tilak and Gandhi. Gandhi always upheld the sacred and unimpeachable right of any individual to oppose a law if it really went against the sacred dictates of his conscience. The whole sociology of Satyagraha rests on the deliberate non-violent efforts for the assertion of a higher law of morality. In South Africa he taught the people to break a law which was calculated to jeopardize their civil rights. In India also he successfully practised civil disobedience on various occasions. V.S. Srinivasa Shastri says, "Left to himself Lokamanya would never break the law openly and invite its rigours like Mahatma Gandhi. Neither is it possible to conceive that he would, like Gandhi, throw down the gage to government and all unarmed, take the vow of victory or death."[52]

Footnotes

1. Tilak, Writing and Speeches, *op. cit.,* p. 250.
2. *Ibid.,* p. 256.
3. Varma, *op. cit.,* p. 179.
4. *Ibid.,* p. 179.
5. *Ibid.*
6. *Ibid.*
7. *Ibid.,* p. 180.
8. Karmarkar, *op. cit.,* p. 134.
9. *Ibid.,* p. 135.
10. *Ibid.,* p. 145.
11. *Ibid.,* p. 149.
12. *Ibid.,* p. 150.
13. Varma, *op. cit.,* pp. 185-86.
14. Karmarkar, *op. cit.,* p. 138.
15. Varma, *op. cit.,* p. 197.
16. Tahmankar, *op. cit.,* p. 114.
17. *Ibid.,* pp. 115-16.
18. Varma, *op. cit.,* p. 205.
19. Tahmankar, *op. cit.,* p. 114.
20. Varma, *op. cit.,* p. 202.
21. Tilak, Writing and Speeches, *op. cit.,* pp. 48-49.
22. Varma, *op. cit.,* p. 194.
23. Tilak, Writing and Speeches, *op. cit.,* p. 36.
24. *Ibid.,* p. 298.
25. Tahmankar, *op. cit.,* p. 116.
26. *Ibid.*
27. Inamdar, *op. cit.,* p. 273.
28. *Ibid.,* p. 277.
29. *Ibid.,* p. 274.
30. *Ibid.*
31. *Ibid.,* p. 277.
32. Varma, *op. cit.,* pp. 446-447.
33. Pradhan and Bhagwat, *op. cit.,* p. 127.
34. *Ibid.,* p. 210.
35. *Ibid.,* p. 128.
36. Varma, *op. cit.,* p. 448.
37. *Ibid.,* p. 448.
38. Pradhan and Bhagwat, *op. cit.,* p. 207
39. I.M. Reisner and N.M. Goldberg, *op. cit.,* p. 656.
40. *Ibid.,* pp. 655-656.
41. *Ibid.,* p. 656.
42. Pradhan and Bhagwat, *op. cit.,* pp. 209-10.

43. H.W. Nevinson, *op. cit.,* p. 76.
44. B.C. Pal, *Indian Nationalism : Its Principles and Personalities,* Madras, S.R. Murthy & Co., 1918, p. 69.
45. *Ibid.,* pp. 71-72.
46. Varma, *op. cit.,* p. 449.
47. T.V. Parvate, *Bal Gangadhar Tilak,* Ahmedabad, Navajivan Publishing House, p. 266.
48. Nevinson, *op. cit.,* pp. 72-73.
49. Varma, *op. cit.,* p. 211.
50. Pal, *op. cit.,* p. 65.
51. Tilak, Writing and Speeches, *op. cit.,* p. 299.
52. Varma, *op. cit.,* p. 451.

7 Nationalism Versus Internationalism

Tilak was a nationalist, but not a narrow nationalist. He had a keen understanding of international affairs and was always conscious about it. He always tried to make a prestigious room on international platform for India. In Indian political thought, narrow nationalism was disparaged and internationalism of some sort was eulogised. The Encyclopaedia Americana says that "There is no incompatibility between liberal nationalism and a spirit of internationalism", because it said that "if kept within reasonable limits, a healthy patriotism is a great spiritual force."[1]

Nationalism in India has always favoured internationalism and opposed imperialism. The national leaders of India have always maintained before them a wider objective of humanity and considered nationalism as a highway to internationalism. Therefore, in India, natioalism has not come in conflict with internationalism. Tilak was a vedantist and he too pleaded for reconciliation between the ideal of nationalism and the vedantic conception of human unity. He states in his 'Gita Rahasya' that love to the country is only a step to broad-based cosmopolitanism and quotes "Vasudhaiva Kutumbakam".

It was natural that Tilak's observations on India's freedom. He constantly sought an answer to the question as to why India had met the fate of a slave nation, and whether this condition was irrevocable? His anser to the second question was an emphatic 'no'.[2] Tilak's perception and evaluation of international events were characterized by two factors. First, his international perspective was conditioned by his struggle for national freedom. Second, he was inclined to think in terems of East-West dichotomy and to view Asian countries as bound together by cultural and historical ties.[3] The first and second decades of 19th century were most crucial periods for the diplomatic world. High tensions were arising between the imperialist powers and the whole world was suffering with them. Tilak, thus, being an intelligent politician and journalist, expressed his views from time to time on different international events in different manners, keeping the position of India always in his mind and its relation and effect with the event.

First World War

Tilak had the international factor always in his mind and he did believe that India's opportunity would come when England was in difficulty, and when such paychological moments arose, Indian people must be mentally prepared and united to catch time by the forelock and carry out their objective. He recognized that here entered a factor which was beyond the Indian people's control and an element of chance or luck entered the whole consideration but when such an opportunity appeared to favour them they must be able to strike while the iron was hot. That was the line of reasoning.[4]

Tilak saw new opportunities for India in the prospect of a prolonged war. He was convinced that each montth the war went on must draw India more and more into the vortex of British politics and that her vast resources in manpower and raw materials must make her indispensable to the Allied victory. After the U.S.A. which England had been courting since the beginning of the war, India was probably the only country which could furnish the Allied powers with raw materials in abundance for the manufacture of munitions.

Tilak therefore argued that to win the war India's help would be vital, this in turn would enhance her prestige and add strength to her demand for her proper place in the counsels of the Empire. In Tilak's view the psychological moment had arrived, and he now decided to go all out to exploit it. He was convinced that India's demands stood a good chance of being conceded by Britain if she made them in the consciousness of her strength and spoke with one voice.[5] Here we see clear difference between Gandhi and Tilak, while Gandhi was ready to support and help Britain without any condition at the point of humanity only, Tilak wanted to support Britain on the condition of assuring self-government for India after the war.

He did believe in the declarations of high-minded British people of making India fit for self-government by planting and promoting representative and democratic insttitutions among Indians, but he also knew tthat besides these liberal and high-minded people, there were conservatives and imperialists, and above all, the bureaucracy in India and its allies and the British vested interests which were opposed to India ever attaining freedom, and therefore conflict with those who held the reins of power was inevitable. He was always on the alert to take full advantage of the conflicts in which popular interests clashed with those of the bureaucracy and its allies to develop people's power of resistance and self-assertion and he did not spare himself in the least.[6]

The outbreak of the first world war was viewed by Tilak also as an opportunity to convince the British Emperor about the bankrupt policies of the bureaucracy in India. He pointed to the fact that in the hour of crisis this bureaucracy could not mobilize more than 4 to 5 lakhs of people for recruitment to the Army, which meant that people in India were not willing to defend their motherland in the face of external danger. And he put the blame for this dismal circumstance squarely on the British government in India. For during its regime of more than hundred years, the British government had run the affairs of this country in a manner which would lead to no other result but the emasculation of all the people. Such was the impact of subjection on the mind of the Indian people. If India was not to become a dead weight on the British empire, the only solution was to grant self-government to its people. After the war was over, Tilak demanded self-government for India, because the war was fought for "making the world safe for democracy", as President Wilson had stated. A new ethos of liberty which had been created, made the continuation of subjection of India basically incompatible.[7] Tilak also demanded for India the same right of representation in the proposed League of Nations and urged to apply the principle of self-determination for India, which was one of the major principles in Wilson's Fourteen Point. When Tilak demanded to apply the principle of self-determination for India, it clearly meant that he was demanding 'Swaraj' for India. Here we see, how intelligently Tilak tried to benefit his country by means of an international event.

Tilak's Memorandum: the Starting Point of Indian Foreign Policy

Tilak sent a memorandum to the Paris Peace Conference, on behalf of the Indian people. In this important memorandum, he referred : "India is self-contained, harbours no design upon the integrity of other states and has no ambition outside India. With her vast areas, enormous resources and prodigious population she may well aspire to be a leading power in Asia if not in the world. She could therefore easily be a powerful steward of the League of Nations in the East for maintaining the peace of the world... With politically enchained India, it is impossible. From the point of view of the peace of Asia and from the point of view of the peace of the world it is, therefore, absolutely necessary that India should be self-governed internally, and be made the bulwark of liberty in the East..."[8]

Thus, we see that Tilak thought that a self-governed India should stand as a pillar of peace in the world. It marked the beginning of the present foreign policy of India. The framework of Indian foreign policy is based on peace specially. Another important thing that Tilak mentioned in the memorandum is that "India is self-contained... and has no ambition outside India." Here we find another important point of our present foreign policy. It indicates that India is against colonisation. We all know that decolonisation is another important basis of our foreign policy. We see here much similarities between the principles of Panchasheel and the ideas of Tilak mentioned in the memorandum. The principles of Panchasheel are :

1. Mutual respect for each other's terriotorial integrity and sovereignty;
2. Mutual non-aggression;
3. Mutual non-interference in each other's internal affairs;
4. Equality and mutual benefit;
5. Peaceful co-existence.[9]

Here it can be said that the first three principles of Panchsheel come within the limit of Tilak's statement :

"India is self-contained and has no ambition outside India." If India is self-contained, then it is natural that she sill be non-aggressive and if she has no ambition outside India, it becomes necessary that she will respect others' terriotrial integrity and sovereignty and a country having these sentiments will never interfere in others' internal affairs. Thus after the analysis of the statements of memorandum we can consider it as the first document of Indian foreign policy. In this very memorandum we can find most of the important principles of our present Indian foreign policy, for example, peace, decolonisation, non-aggression and non-interference.

The Turkey Problem and Khilafat Movement

On the question of Turkey, Tilak had whole-heartedly supported the Mohammedan demand that the Ottoman Empire must be left untouched and the holy institution of the Khilafat kept inviolate. Not only did he believe that the religious feelings of the Muslims in this matter should be respected by Britain and France, but he also considered that in order to maintainthe balance of power in the Middle East, Turkey should at all costs remain strong and independent.[10] He looked at the question of Turkey from the standpoint of a political realist. He considered that the independence of Turkey was as important to India as the independence of France and Belgium on the continent was to the British Isles. While Gandhi's support of the Khilafat agitation was mainly emotional and moral, Tilak's support was based on a more stable foundation consideration of the defence of India and her relations with the Middle Eastern countries. Discussing this aspect of Turekey's independence with his friend, Gangadharrao Deshpande, Tilak said : "The British have won the war and therefore they are no longer afraid that the Muslims of India will rise in rebellion. British is now playing for high stakes in the Middle East. By undermining or destroying the Turkish Empire she wants to control all the Muslim countries which are neighbours of India. It is in the interest of India that the Muslim power of Turkey should remain undiminshed. I think the idea of helping the Muslims in their Khilafat agitation is a sound one and Mahatma Gandhi's lead in this matter should be supported by all." From this it is clear that Tilak supported Khilafat agitation not only from a sentimental point of view, but he was thinking about its impact on international politics and specially its effect on India's polittical future.

Sino-Japanese War

Tilak paid tributes to Japan for her victory over China and stated that this was possible because of Japan's achievements in terms of modernization. He expressed his surprise over the fact that a tiny nation like Japan could easily defeat China with its gigantic territory, population and resources. Surprise and appriciation for Japan's rapid progress were natural feelings for anyone who in those days witnessed the dismal spectacle of the whole of Asia lying prostrate before the European powers. Japan's emergence as a modern power certainly created a hope among Asians that afterall, they were not inexorably consigned to the fate of slavery and that if they, like the Japanese, took to modern ways, they too could reverse the tide of history. But after having said all this, it remained a fact that Japan's action against China could not be described in any other terms than imperialism. And one could have expected Tilak, who did not lose a single opportunity for opposing British imperial rule in India, to disapprove Japanese action. But instead of disapproving it, Tilak thought it fit tto praise Japan which, in his opinion, had done great service to China by exposing here weakness and thus creating a possibility of resurgence in China,[12] so that China would not continue to sleep in the same way as before. In an article in the Kesari on 14th May, 1895, Tilak analysed the causes of China's downfall and Japan's rise : "The Chinese people are intelligent, talented and skilful but they have not prospered because they seem to have made a resolve, as it were, to stick to their traditional, social and political system... A few years ago Japan also was like China, but then light dawned upon the people of Japan in time; they made the desired changes in their conduct of life, in their social and political systems. The present victory, in spite of the comparative smallness of the country in area, population and resources, is an important event in the history of the world. This war is bound to give a new form to the history of the world. Russia, England and France have begun to realise that they have now an enemy of equal might to contend with." As for the lesson that India could learn from the rise of Japan, Tilak said that "The lesson taught by Japan to India is not a small one." He compared India with China and remarked that "India is like China : intelligent, considerate, but too fond of sleep", and this was a great demerit for a country like India. He said that "If we stick to our religious or social prejudices and do not allow knowledge, conducive to warfare, enter our minds, we shall never rise. If we leave aside our intransigence, tread warily to grasp knowledge wherever possible, we shall learn to act in concert, learn discipline and self-control, adventure and industry. Japan has shown us that our salvation lies in imitating the European nations judiciously. If we fail to grasp this lesson, we shall get as great a blow as China."[13] Tilak thus fully realised the significance of this war and he saw, in the victory won by Japan, the dawn of a new era for India.

Russia-Japan War

Tilak welcomed the Japanese victory over Russia in the battle of Mikaden. For him, the battle was not simply between two powers. It was a historic battle which had decided the fundamental issues of the West versus East. Tilak argued that there was not something inherent in the nature of Asians which made them unworthy of independent national life but their loss of freedom was only the rsult of their ignorance of modern methods of warfare. Thus the myth of intrinsic inferiority of Asians was exploded by the Japanese victory.[14]

Against European Imperialism

By the turn of the nineteenth century the imperialist rivalry among European powers had became intense. This was reflected in the diplomatic manoeuvres for making and remaking alliances. While Russia came close to France for checkmating Britain, Germany unsuccessfully sought alliance with Britain; Britain in her turn joined hands with Japan for containing Russian advance in the Far East. The German concern was with the prevention of Russian hand in the Balkans and with possibility of German penetration of the whole region from Constanttinople to the Persian Gulf. Reviewing these imperialist moves and counter-moves in Afganistan, Iran, China, Indo-China, Tibet and Asia Minor, Tilak posed a vital question as to whether the destinies of the whole continent of Asia would remain in the hands of the ancient societies, or would pass, as in the case of America and Africe, into hands of the Christian nations. For the first time in world history, he said, the grim spectre of all Asian people meeting the same fate as that of Indians, has been raised. In this critical hour, Indian people naturally felt a sense of solidarity with all Asian societies as against the impending danger of European onslaught.[15]

Conclusion

Tilak was not only a political leader but an intelligent diplomat having deep international insight. He always measured all the international events from Indian point of view, whether it was the Sino-Japanese war, Turkey problem or First World War. The memorandum which he prepared for the Paris Peace Conference indicates his dynamic knowledge of future and world politics. This is why, we find many principles of our present foreign policy in this very document. Tilak knew that India has to face so many problems in the post-independence period and those problems could not be solved without peaceful conditions. World peace is the condition which enables a nation to plan for prosperity. A state of war will not allow agriculture and industries to prosper. Peace is therefore a basic necessity for the development of backward countries.[16] Tilak knew this fact and this was the reason, why he wanted to see the self-governed India as a messenger of peace in the world, because peace was the first and foremost condition for the development and prosperity of independent India.

Tilak had felt that the efforts for the mobilization of public opinion in favour of India's independence should be extended beyond India's frontiers. He encouraged and helped Lala Lajpat Rai and others in such endeavours in the U.S.A. and European countries. He appeared to have great faith in the efficacy of the newly set up League of Nations. He believed that the statesmen in Europe and U.S.A. had created the League as a unique constitutional instrument to preserve and promote liberty and peace in the world. He was writing in the second year of the League's existence, that is at a time when there prevailed an atmosphere of great optimism regarding the future world order. It was natural that Tilak was also influenced by this atmosphere. Tilak thought that the great war and its end in victory for Britain and her allies had created a favourable international atmospher for the cause of India's freedom. Was it not a fact that a very costly war had been waged against Germany because she had tried to subjugate small nations like Belgium, Serbia and Rumania? If Britain had relentlessly fought to preserve independence and liberty in the world, it would be incongruous for her not to grant liberty and independence to India. Tilak felt that the statesmen in Britain had started thinking in these terms. Before the international atmosphere slided back to the pre-war stage, Tilak wanted India to make a decisive bid for independence.[17]

Footnotes

1. *Encyclopaedia Americana (Vol. 19)*, New York, American Corporation International Headquarters, pp. 757-765.
2. Inamdar, *op. cit.*, p. 146.
3. *Ibid.*, p. 143.
4. Parvate, *op. cit.*, p. 269.
5. Tahmankar, *op. cit.*, p. 228.
6. Parvate, *op. cit.*, p. 269-70.
7. Inamdar, *op. cit.*, p. 148.
8. *Samagra Lokamanya Tilak (Vol. 7) Towards Independence*, Poona, Kesari Prakashan, pp. 264-65.
9. C. P. Bhambhri, *Foreign Policy of India*, New Delhi, Sterling Publishers Private Limited, p. 12.
10. Tahmankar, *op. cit.*, p. 303.
11. *Ibid.*
12. Inamdar, *op. cit.*, p. 145.
13. Pradhan and Bhagwar, *op. cit.*, pp. 96-97.
14. Inamdar, *op. cit.*, pp. 146-47.
15. *Ibid.*, p. 146.
16. Murthy, *op. cit.*, p. 23.
17. Inamdar, *op. cit.*, pp. 149-50.

8 Tilak and the Modern Age

Every personis the representative of his own age. But there are some people who not only represent their own age, but become the torch-bearer for the future. Tilak was one among them. In the beginning of his career, Tilak was more concerned with social works than with the political. He used traditional and religious bases of Indian nationalism. Even before Tilak, religion had been an important factor for the social nationalists, like Ram Mohan Roy, Vidyasagar and Vivekanand. Religion had indeed been an essential ingradient of nationalism in all the phases of Indian nationalism, even after Tilak. Gandhi, who in the post-Tilak period provided mass base to Indian independence, was essentially a religious person. Gandhi used to chant prayers not only in the private but in mass meetings regularly. Gandhi's popular prayer bracketed Ishwar (i.e. Hindu god) with Allan (i.e. Muslim god) invoking the idea that God is similar for all religions. In his mass meetings, Hindus, Muslims or Christians present there chanted the prayer - "Raghupati Raghav Raja Ram" - without having the feeling that they were signing a song which eulogised Ram, the Hindu deity. Gandhi had, in fact, got Ram accepted as the cultural ancestor of all Indians. Ram's symbol was the common heritage of all Indians as no other religion existed at the time Ram's songs were sung in the Indus valley civilization. However, Gandhi was always characterized as a secular man; it is important to prove why Tilak was not regarded as secular while Gandhi was. Tilak used Hindu symbols as Gandhi also did. Tilak, like Gandhi, never criticised other religions or he never preached hatred against any other religion. Religion has not been fully isolated from nationalism. As Tapan Raychoudhary says, "In modern times, nationhood has inspired such loyalties as were commanded only by religion inearlier ages. Indeed it has taken the place of religion, for vast sections of mankind."[1]

Tilak was also a sympathiser of other values which became prominent later. After independence, we know that socialism and secularism have become an essential factor of Indian nationalism. As far as secularism is concerned, we can say that the present secular nationalism, which is a gift to the nation specially of Nehru, is quite different from the nationalism of Tilak. Tilak's nationalism can be characterized as traditional nationalism. Tilak wanted to raise the self-respect of the Indian people by recalling the immortal values of Indian tradition. He conveyed his solid ideas to the people by referring to the Gita ideal of Karma-yoga.[2] According to Tilak, the knowledge of Indian tradition was necessary for each and every Indian, because he knew that it was only the tradition which makes the national character. He was a democrat, thus he knew that national character is necessary for the success of democracy. When an administration is run directly or indirectly by the people, its national character must be of a high level.[3]

Tilak gave more emphasis on the building of national character and for this purpose he used religious symbols and incidents in his speeches or writings. If it is called Hindu nationalism then here is a question — Is religion synonymous with commualism? It is difficult to agree with this view, even though religious symbols, mythology and terminology are widely used in communal argumentation. Religion or its practice may be condemned with logical justification from the standpoint of rationalism, atheism or scientific approach, but to recommend its abolition as a means of eradicating communalism is barking up the wrong tree. The very way of life of the Indian people refutes the argument. The overwheliming majority of them believes in some religion and to say that all of them, or even a significant number of them, are communal would be unfounded.[4] This is not only true for the common people, but also of the leaders. Nobody could ever accuse Mahatma Gandhi, Maulana Azad, Dr. Ansari or Purshottam Das Tandon of having communal tendencies, though all of them were deeply religious in their lives. On the other hand the personalities associated with the communal movements are not known for any kind of attachment to religions which they claimed to defend or promote. Mohammad Ali Jinnah is the most outstanding example of a thoroughly secular person espousing a communal cause.[5]

The core of religion is its spirituality, its philosophy of life, birth and death, its quest for ultimate reality supranatural and metaphysical. The communal approach has not even a remote relationship to any such thing. It concerns itself exclusively with the 'here' and not hereafter, with things mundane rather than spiritual. It makes no attempt at religious-social reform or innovation to harmonise religious belief with scientifically discovered facts or laws of life is none of its concerns. The communalist comes into action only when there is an opportunity to move or mobilize the followers of faith against an usually imaginary threat, as happened recently with regard to conversions. Justice to Harijans was no priority for those who organized massive summelans in defence of Hinduism. If it were, the cause should have been taken up long ago. It was taken up only as a hot issue capable of evoking the sympathy of a large section of caste Hindus and instilling in them a fear of their identity as Hindus being overwhelmed by the Muslims.[6] There is hardly any instance of a truly religious person being intolerant of other faiths or beliefs. Hazarat Mohammad enjoined upon his followers respect for the prophets and holy men of other religions and regions. Krishna, the incarnation of Vishnu, told Arjuna that all roads in pursuit of truth would ultimately lead to 'Him'. Even the pursuit of politics in the spirit of religion, as exemplified by Mahatma

Gandhi, did not admit of hatred, ill-will or rancour against the adversary.[7]

From the communal angle religion is more a line of demarcation, a mark of identity, asserting differences and separation from other groups, than a spiritual approach tending to obliterate identities and inspiring realization of unity in diversity, the one in many, or a force enabling one to perfectly harmonise one's self with the society, the environment and the cosmos. Religion in the hands of a communalist is divested of all that makes it vital and eternal; it is reduced to a slogan, a symbol, and instrument to excite passions or to obscure reason, an opiate or a heady wine. The communal approach of secularizing religion by laying emphasis on its national and ephemeral identification marks is basically in contradiction with the religious approach as reflected in the attitudes of the great practitioners of spirituality and also in the attitudes of the vast mass of population who adhere to it as a framework of values that brings order to social life. The poser communal versus secular or secular versus religious is misplaced and not valid.[8]

Our present secular nationalism has no close connection with Indian traditions. This is why, a nationalism as intense in its appeal was not absent in India in the early decades of Independence but it is no part of our political emotions today in any significant way. The feeble propaganda in the cause of national unity and appeals in the name of nation projected by the state or T.V. soap operas do not alter the situation.[9] Loyalties, idealism, the willingness to die for a cause, all these are far from absent in our public life today. The multiple public passions blazing all over the territory are not inspired by the nation state to establish which earlier generations made massive sacrifices.[10] These all are happening, because Indians are going far from their traditions.

We can see two kinds of propagandists nowadays here and there in the society. The one favour secularism; this group of people presents itself as more modernly educated and polite in the society and the other group favoures a certain religion, whether it is Hindu, Muslim or any other. These people are called communalists by the secularists of the society. But the matter of fact is that if we carefully study the ideas of both of the groups, we find an amazing factor, that the majority of these people does not know the real meaning of religion. Tilak wanted to teachthis real meaning of religion to the people by recalling the high values of Indian traditions. He never was an advocate of religious nationalism.

Here is an example of Dushanabe : General Gozi was addressing a meeting of about 10 thousand enthusiastic people on 7th May, 1992. He asked them, "do you want ?" The crowd cried - 'Islam, Islam'. 'Do you want an Islamic state'? asked Gozi. The crowd cried — 'Yes, Yes'.[11]

This is an example of religious nationalism, but there is not a single example of this kind of incident in any of the meetings of Tilak He was a philosopher and always used 'religion' in a philosophic and broad sense. If we see his explanation on 'Dharma' in 'Gita-Rahasya' we can easily come to know what religion was in his opinion. However, if we think dispassionately, it seems that secularism itself is a confusing phenomenon. We can hardly find a man having equal loyalty to all the religions. It is natural for a person to have some more love or respect in his heart for a particular religion, to which he belongs, and keeping this love in his heart, he will never disturb the persons of other religion or make good relations with them. If this is secularism, then why Tilak was not secular?

Sep. 1992. Our former President Shankar Dayal Sharma said on the occasion of Ganapati festival in Maharashtra in September 1992. Ganapati is the God of democracy, and this is why he wants to worship him for the sake of the country. This raises an important question : if a supreme head of a secular democratic republic worships Ganapati as a God of democracy and no one is going to blame him that his speech is against secularism then why Tilak was not secular or why Tilak was a religious nationalist when he did the same work. Once late Rajiv Gandhi defined secular India as 'a religious country, in which all religions are respected equally'.[12] Narasimha Rao also says that 'secularism does not mean religionalessness', but no one is going to call him an unsecular man, then there is no question to characterize Tilak as an unsecular person.

Coming to socialism, we do not find Tilak to have sympathies for Lenin, his contemporary in Russia. But in a broad sense Tilak was a sympathiser of the poor. Tilak presented himself as a well-wisher of all the sections of society. Services done by him from time to time for the society, physically and through his writings too, have been immense. His appeal to the educated was : You are the natural leader of the masses. You must go to their cottages, understand them, organize them, and help them to improve their conditions. It is foolish to regard ourselves as different from the people, because we have learnt a few books. We are one of them and must remain in their midst."[13] Writing on the eve of the eleventh session of the Congress in 1906, he said, "We must so define our policy and programme as to induce workers and agriculturists to join the Congress and enthuse them to implement its resolution."[14]

In 1902, he said, "The real condition of India must be studied not in the cities but amongst the workers and peasants inthe country. India is our motherland, all Indians are brethren and our mission is to ameliorate their political and social condition."[15] One can say that Tilak did not speak in terms of conflict of interests of workers and capitalists. But from what Tilak said and did, it is clear that he initiated the idea of consensus and harmony of interests of all the people and sections of the society which Gandhi and Nehru carried forward. Tilak too expressed himself in favour of villages. If Gandhi said that 'The soul of India lies in the villages', he echoed Tilak's idea.

As one of the secretaries of Bombay Provincial Conference in 1890, Tilak used to propagate the idea that only educated men should not meet once in a year and say all they wanted in the name of the people. In an article in the Kesari in that year he said: "The Government will not grant any request if only some 500 people gather together once a year as self-chosen delegates and make a petition. That will be a weighty petition if only it is supported by similar petitions from the provinces, districts, towns and villages. Before a united demand is presented from the Congress platform it must arise from beneath. When this natural course will be followed and decisions will not be taken from top, we will be fit for exercise of democratic rights and to run representative institutions and Government will listen to us as real representative of the people."[16] Tilak was a progenitor of the idea of democratic decentralization of power. Therefore, his idea was : 'decisons will not be taken from the top'. He wanted all the classes of society to join in the work of nation-building and improvement. Thus, it is a matter of inquiry, was Tilak a supporter of democratic socialism?

Tilak and Gandhi both were a democrat but we find a big difference between the two. Gandhi was a supporter of democratic idealism. Tilak and Gandhi both were against fraud in diplomacy; but if the opponent was a supporter of this kind of diplomacy, Tilak had no hesitation to use it in return, but Gandhi did not do like this. He always followed his method of idealism; whether the opponent was ideal or fraud. Tilak was an ardent follower of Gita which teaches us to act according to the demand of time. Now, this is a questin of inquiry : was Tilak more useful than Gandhi for the modern age, because the demand of the modern age politics is very much similar to Tilak than Gandhi?

Footnotes

1. Tapan Raychoudhary, *The Sunday Times,* 26th Jan. 1992.
2. Bhola Prasad Verma Shastri, *Hindustan,* 15th Aug. 1992.
3. Yogesh Chandra Sharma, *Hindustan,* 15th Aug. 1992.
4. Asghar Ali Engineer (ed.) *Communal Riots in Post Independence India,* Hyderabad, Sangam Books India (Pvt.) Ltd., 1984, pp. 43-44.
5. *Ibid.,* p. 44.
6. *Ibid.,* pp. 44-45.
7. *Ibid.,* p. 45

8. *Ibid.*
9. Raychoudhary, *op. cit.*
10. *Ibid.*
11. M. J. Akbar, *Hindustan,* 19th May, 1992.
12. India's Rajiv : A Film by Simi Garewal.
13. Parvate, *op. cit.,* p. 267.
14. *Ibid.*
15. *Ibid.*
16. *Ibid.,* pp. 266-67.

9 Conclusion

There are two types of nationalism : in both, nationalism is primarily a cultural phenomenon, although it often takes a political form. One is the nationalism of the enlightenment which was by and large rational rather than emotional and the other based on culture and traditions. It can be said that Tilak's nationalism was the mixture of both types of nationalism. This examination of Tilak's concept of nationalism finds that his nationalism was both rational as well as cultural and traditional.

Tilak's conception of nationalism was a combination of the vedanta ideal of the spiritual unity of mankind and the western notions of nationalism. He was influenced by the development of nationalism throughout the world. Tilak's concept of 'Swaraj' was to a great extent rational. It was neither a product of romantic nationalism, nor of spiritual nationalism. The thrust of his argument in favour of 'Swaraj' basically was not emotional. He preferred to elaborate the adverse moral and material efforts of British rule, and then render a rational explanation of this phenomenon. Tilak used 'dharma' only with a view to emphasize that Swaraj was not only a natural right of the people but also a bounden duty, a sort of moral obligation. It did not have any religious implications. He did not explain the 'Gita' only for intellectual luxury, nor he did it as a religious duty or as a religious preacher, but he referred to Gita to emphasize the philosophy of rationalism alongwith that of Indian traditions and through this, he wanted to revoke the Indian masses for their supreme action — the attainment of Swaraj. He strengthened the basis of Indian nationalism by giving the evidence of Vedas. He proved in the 'Arctic Home in the Vedas' that the Aryan civilization was one of the most ancient civilizations in the world and from this argument, it becomes clear that the Hindu culture was one of the oldest cultures in the world. Though his argument in the 'Arctic Home in the Vedas' strengthens the basis of Hindu nationalism, it is not fair to regard him as a Hindu nationalist. It is true that he was a Hindu by religion and he was an admirer of Hindu traditions but it did not mean that he was against Muslims or any other religion. Many of the Muslim leaders were blind followers of Tilak. Hinduism was the uniting force of the country, for Tilak. He thought that Hindu epics had forged unity of thought and conduct among the citizens of India as a whole.

Tilak concentrated not only on the cultural and religious bases of nationalism but also on the economic basis of it. He shared the economic ideas of the moderate nationalists like Ranade, Naoroji, R.C. Dutt and Gokhale. But, according to him economic issues had to be exploited to rouse the people's political consciousness and strengthen the freedom struggle. For this purpose, he wrote several articles in his vernacular journal, Kesari, on such issues as land revenue, land tenure system, the destruction of arts and crafts, the wasteful government expenditure on wars and the conspicuous living of British officials. He endorsed Dadabhai Naoroji's famous 'drain theory' of British rule in India. He gave a favourable picture of the native regimes of India, contrasted with exploitative rule of the imperialists. He, thereby, made out a case for replacing foreign rule by Home Rule. Though he shared Ranade's concern for the industrialization of India, he was against his defence of British rule for its role in industrial investment and development of transport, communication and trade. Tilak also shared R.C. Dutt's anxiety over the deteriorating rural situation evident in recurring famines and the growing indebtedness of the farmers. He advocated a greater role of the state in agricultural development. He was not moderate in his outlook like Dutt, but he was a complete extremist.

Tilak knew that the bases of nationalism were both objective and subjective. Such objective factors as common language, territory and religion contribute to the psychological or subjective feeling of oneness among the people. These subjective, psychological feelings are indeed of fundamental importance for nationalism. Tilak believed that nationalism can be promoted and strengthened if people's psychological bonds are given symbolic expressions of an objective, visible and concrete type, namely, flags, insignia and celebration of social and religious festivals. This is why, he revived the Ganapati festival. This festival was the symbol of the activist protest movement and an attempt to bridge the gap between the elite leaders and general people, as well as the Brahmins and the non-Brahmins. The other intention to celebrate this festival was to unite the different classes of society on one platform.

Similarly he also played a leading role in organizing Shivaji festivals. Political festivals were necessary according to him and unfortunately there was lack of political festivals in India at that time. He stressed the necessity of honouring the great national heroes, because festivals for the great leaders and martyrs of the country had a vitalizing role in the work of national emancipation. He wanted that the Shivaji festival would spread in the whole of the country without any distinction of caste and creed. He encouraged the Muslims also to participate in the celebration of this national festival, because love of nation was the foremost duty of every person; although he said that they were not bound to participate in the worship. He said that Shivaji had been born in very critical times and the country had been again passing through similar periods of crises and it was therefore essential that Shivaji's spirit should be followed. He stressed the necessity of a leader like Shivaji in that time who could regenerate the country by his self-sacrifice, ardent devotion and disinterested action.

Tilak was not a supporter of violence but if anyone committed violence for a (purified aim), then he did not use to hate him. This is why, he justified the murder of Afzal Khan by Shivaji, because Shivaji murdered Afzal Khan not for his personal interest but for the interest fo his country. Thus Tilak did not use to hate those people who used violent measures for a just cause. Shivaji was not against any caste or race, but he was against the administrative system of that time. Tilak was also not against the British race or Christian religion, but he was against the British colonial system. He wanted to recall the ideal of Shivaji to the people to make them ready to fight with the British bureaucracy. He was an ardent follower of Gita and he had no hesitation to oppose the unjust steps of the British government.

Tilak always used to say that Muslims were not alien in India, but he was against the partial policy of British government to satisfy the Muslims and brand the Hindus as seditionaists. He always said that there were three parties concerned in the Hindu-Muslim dispute; the Hindus, the Muslims and the British government. He was against the caste or communal representation because according to him the true eligibility for voting and representation should be a minimum educational standard and an income level and not considerations of caste and community. Tilak had the foresight to see, how dangerous the communal and caste representation was for the society and he, therefore, opposed that as the basis of representation.

Tilak was absolutely against the bureaucracy under the British regime because it acted to serve colonial interests of the British government. He wanted to obtain a large share in the administration of the country, but he knew that it was hopeless to expect anything from the bureaucracy. Therefore, the only way was that the people should show that they were fit for privileges. Answering the plea of the bureaucracy that the Indians were not yet fit for the share in the administration, he said that if Indians were not fit to obtain the share in administration, hone but the bureaucracy was responsible for it. Very wisely he always referred to the fact that Indians were not against the English people, English institutions, English liberty and the Empire, but they were against the then bureaucracy, and demanded that the internal administration of India should be under Indian control. He said that the Indians had to convince the Government that the country could not be governed well by the present method and the present bureaucracy was not serving the interests of the Indian people; so it must be removed.

Tilak said that the bureaucracy was not the Government. There is a difference between the bureaucracy and the Government and his fight was against the bureaucracy and not with the Government, because it was bureaucracy which was responsible for the implementation of the decisions of the Government. He remarked that the bureaucracy was not serving the interests of Indian people and that was the reason the Indians were against the bureaucracy. He urged the Government to restrict the repressive methods of the bureaucracy. At the time of his historic trial, he fearlessly confessed before the jury that he was representing a great struggle between the bureaucracy and the people of India and but it was not sedition to point out the demerits and defaults of the bureaucracy.

Tilak could not understand why Indians were not fit to rule themselves while they showed their ruling ability at several ocassions in the past. The great rulers like Ashoka, Guptas and Rajputs had shown how to rule. Then why Indians were not fit at present when they had been so in the past. There was no disqualification, intellectual or physical, which disabled the Indians from taking part in the Government or in the administration. They had shown their fitness in the past and were prepared to show it under the British regime also if opportunities were granted to them. Even with the few opportunities that they got, they showed their ability and had always come up to the standard of efficiency required. About the British argument that certain British interests would suffer in the event of Home Rule,

Tilak replied that the British interests would be safeguarded so far as justice and law were concerned, because Indians did not want anarchy but peace and good government.

Tilak was a leader of masses and thus, he wanted the participation of every class of the society in the national movement, whether they were students, peasants or workers. He was against the moderates' view that students should not take part in the national movement, and instead should confine themselves to the academic world. Tilak's argument was that this ideal was suited for normal peaceful times, but when the country was engaged in a furious struggle with the bureaucracy, students should do something to help national movement, and if the teachers stood against the students, because of their participation in the national movement, they should be disobeyed by the students. Similarly, the agriculturists and the workers also should take part in the national movement. He pointed out that they should take part in the activities of the Congress also, because it was necessary for the success of a national party or institution to be deep-rooted in the feelings and sentiments of masses. He was against this view that the important decisions of Congress would be taken by the educated class only. He wanted that the educated people should go to villages and train the masses for the national struggle. This was an important duty of the educated class. They were more learned than the ordinary people, therefore, their responsibility was also more than that of the ordinary people. He said that the educated class was also a part of the society and their interests were also same as the other classes of society. If one considered himseif extraordinary and different from the society because he was an educated person, then he was going on a wrong way. The educated people should mix with the masses, and work with them. Only then the struggle for freedom would be fight in a real sense. He said that the petition of the Congress could become weighty only when it would be supported by all the provinces, districts, towns and villages of the country, because a demand became powerful only when it arose from beneath. he was a great admirer of the decentralization of power and always used to say that decisions should not be taken from the top. He wanted to give a mass base to the Congress and a democratic direction to its functioning. His own political activities were directed to the creation of two thought-currents and sentiments among the masses. In the first place, he wanted to promote the spirit of nationalism, which could enable people to transcend the limits of caste and religion and stand as one unit against the foreign domination. Secondly, he was creating among the masses a consciousness of their political rights and was teaching them the new and modern method of criticising and peacefully fighting against political injustice.

According to some critics, Tilak was an orthodox, on the plea that he was an orthodox, on the plea that he was against the social reforms like the Age of Consent Bill etc. Here again the fact remains that Tilak was not against social reform or it didn't mean that he favoured child marriage, but he opposed the Bill because he saw it as the interference of an alien government in the Indian customs. He himself married his daughters not before the age of eighteen, but he did not want to surrender the area of social field, which was under the control of the people, to the control of an alien government. He opposed the Sharda Sadan also, but again it didn't mean that he was against female education. He educated his daughters upto graduation, but he was against the proselytizing activities of the Sadan. He was an experienced leader, thus he knew it well that social reforms could not be practised by legislation. Education, in the real sense, was necessary among the people, for the success of social reforms. He wanted to gain political independence for India at first, because he knew that no reform could become successful in a dependent country. He cited the example of Burma and Ceylon. Both Ceylon and Burma were socially for more advanced than India, but they were politically in the same boat, because their national awakening came much later. Therefore, the prime need of that time was concentration of energy for the attainment of political rights. Social reform would come after political rights had been obtained.

"Education and not legislation was the remedy of social evils", according to Tilak. This is why he put stress on the idea of national education. He did his best to improve the educational standard of his countrymen. For this purpose he started the New English School, Poona and Fergusson College at Poona, and through these institutions he wanted to give national education to the people. These institutions were nursery of Indian nationalism in the real sense. He thought that national education alone can educate the Indians in the real sense, because they lost their national character during the long period of subjugation and it could not be recalled without national education. The English educational system could not be able to teach the countrymen about the rich cultural tradition and national heritage of their country. He also stressed the necessity of a national language, because it was necessary for the unity of the linguistically divided India and Hindi, written in Devanagari script, could only be the national language of India, according to him. He also started to publish two newspapers named 'Kesari' and "Mahratta" for the political awakening of the people. These papers became amazingly popular among the countrymen. The papers were the mouthpiece of Tilak and essays and editorials written by him in the papers were the sources of political inspiration for the public. Specially, the Kesari can be said to have become synonymous with the extremist school of nationalistic politics led by Tilak.

Tilak was an advocate of the freedom of press. He wanted the same type of freedom for the Indian press also, as was given in Britain to the British press. Britain was famous as a nation having respect for the freedom of press. The British press was enjoying this liberty. Therefore, Tilak could not understand why Indian press was denied this liberty. It was the duty of a newspaper man to express his views fearlessly and impartially on every subject and it was possible only when the freedom of expression was given to him. The motive of newspapers was not to earn money only. The papers were started to discuss current topics and public questions and for creating public opinion in the country. He said that if an incident took place on a day, then as a newspaper editor it was his bounden duty to express his views on that very incident in his newspaper on next day. This was the duty of every newspaper man to express his views on every important incident and question at every time, whether the times were excited or peaceful. If a paper did not perform this duty, it means it failed to perform the real duty of a newspaper. Freedom of expression was very important for Tilak. He said that the Indian papers had every right to place their views before the Government, because they were the mouthpiece of the Indian people.

Though Tilak was not in favour of social reforms through legislation by the British government, he was always ready to serve people, physically and economically, whenever they were in distress. He appeared like a legend for the people during the time of plague and famine. During the famine he himself went from shop to shop in the grain market of Poona, requesting shopkeepers not to sell grain at too high price to the poor people. Going into the causes of famine, Tilak said that it was because Indian trade was monopolised by Britain, that the pressure on land had increassed and agriculture was made unproductive. The officials also were too highly paid. It was true that lack of rain caused famine, but it was also true that the people of India had not the strengrth to fight the evil. The poverty of India was wholly due to the repressive policy of the British bureaucracy. Kesari also sounded timely notes of warning against the slow-moving of the officials and insufficient relief works and requested the Government to pay more attention towards the famine-stricken areas.

Tilak's humanitarian activities during the plague were very significant. They showed him to be a constructive political genius of the highest order. When the epidemic appeared in Poona, many of the so-called intellectual leaders and social workers left the town, but Tilak was a firm believer in the immotality of the soul as preached in the Gita and he could not abandon his responsibility at this critical moment. He knew that the spirit of self-sacrifice is the highest criterion of spirituality and spirituality does not mean isolation and deindividualization. It means the transcendence of egoistic interests and requires the spirit of self-sacrifice for the highest ideal of human welfare. Tilak was ready to risk death and disaster in the plague but did not flee away from Poona. He opened the Hindu Plague Hospital in Poona and also a free kitchen in the segregation camp. He established a grainshop also for those who were kept away from the city. He did not care about his personal safety and moved among the people fearlessly and comforted them. He wrote a number of articles in Kesari and Mahratta in which he analysed the different aspects of this great disaster and stressed the necessity of co-operation on a large scale. He also warned the Government not to be oppressive and ruthless in the execution of its policy, because the soldiers who had been employed to enforce the anti-plague measures of the Government were entirely ignorant of the traditions and customs of the local people. He advised also that some of the methods and technics of western medical science could be successfully utilized in fighting the plague.

Tilak was a revolutionary, according to some critics. But there is no concrete evidence to prove him a revolutionary. It is true that he didn not rule out the possibilities of revolution, but as a practical politician he knew it well that the real time of revolution had not yet come. He was not a supporter of men like Ajit Singh, whose theory was based on simple arithmetic that the Indians were much more in number than the British; therefore, sacrificing themselves in a spirit of dedication Indians certainly could destroy the British one by one, and there would be none left in India. He knew that the people of India were not ready for a complete revolution at that time and if they tried to risk rebellion, people would not be ready to join them. He regarded it his responsibility to prevent any hasty or sentimental action. He always advised the young men to work with patience because mangoes should not be gathered before they ripe. He was an experienced leader and thus he knew that a legal and peaceful agitation was better than an unsuccessful revolution, because if a revolution would become unsuccessful, no other revolution could take place for a long time. This condition was very harmful for the freedom struggle of India. Therefore, instead of taking the risk of an unsuccessful revolution, it was better to rely upon the legal political agitation. It is true that Tilak did not hate the revolutionaries and he had good relations with some revolutionaries but he was never a member of any revolutionary society or association nor did he ever advise an armed revolution in his mass meetings or writings.

Tilak harboured a belief in constitutionalism, rule of law, individual freedom, liberty and rights, well-entrenched in a liberal democracy and a limited role of the state in social and economic spheres. He was not an internationalist and a narrow nationalist too. He wanted self-government for India and in his opinion, a self-governed India could be a bastion of liberty in the world. He was against colonialism. He referred in the memorandum which he sent to the Paris Peace Conference that a self-governed India would be a self-contained nation and she should not have any ambition outside the country. This is why Tilak's ideas are suggested to be a starting point of the present Indian foreign policy.

Tilak was a practical leader, so he did not believe in paper works only. He was a man of action and only favoured those works, reforms and legislations which could be practised in the country in the situation of that time. Time has proved how far Tilak was correct. Today we can see that India is independent but there are so many social evils and problems in the country and many of them are not new but are continuing even before the period of Tilak. Tilak was against the fraud in diplomacy, but if the opponent applied it, he had no hesitation to apply it in return. He was a clear-sighted man. He wanted to put his ideas, towards the society strongly and clearly. He was very strict with his principles and never was ready to make any adjustment with his principles. On the whole, we can say that people like Tilak are the pride of our society. He was a great scholar, mathematician, leader, a hard social worker, a real politician and over all a supreme Karmayogi. Only through such leaders the country could advance towards the path of peace and prosperity.

Bibliography

Books

Athalyo, D.V., The Life of Lokamanya Tilak, Poona, Sadashiv Peth, 1921.

Apter, D.E., The Politics of Modernization, Chicago, University of Chicago Press, 1965.

Azad, Abul Kalam, India Wins Freedom, Calcutta, Orient Longman, 1960.

American Corporation International Head Quarters, New York (Publishers), Encyclopaedia Americana, Vol.

Banerjea, Surendranath, The Nation in Making, Bombay, Oxford University Press.

Besant, Annie, India Bond or Free? A World Problem, London, G.P. Putnam & Sons.

Bhambhri, C.P., Foreign Policy of India, New Delhi, Sterling Publishers Private Limited.

Bose, Subhas Chandra, The Indian Struggle, 1920-1934, London, Wishart and Co. Ltd., 1935

Brown, D.M., The Nationalist Movement, Bombay, Jaico Publishing House.

Batten, Edward, Nationalism Politics and Economics, London, P.S. King & Sons Ltd.

Bapat, A.P. and Bros., Poona (Publishers), India in Mourning.

Chandra, Bipan, The Rise and Growth of Economic Nationalism in India, Delhi, People's Publishing House.

Chandra, Sudhir, Dependence and Disillusionment, Delhi, Manas Publications.

Chatterjee, Partha, Nationalist Thought and Colonial World, Oxford University Press.

Chavan, R.S, Nationalism in Asia, New Delhi, Sterling Publishers Pvt. Ltd.

Choudhary, Sukhbir, Growth of Nationalism in India, Vol. I, 1857-1918, New Delhi, Trimurti Publications Pvt. Ltd.

Chirol, Valentine, India, London, Ernest Benn Limited 1926.

Desai, A.R., Social Background of Indian Nationalism, Bombay, Popular Book Depot.

Desai, Morarji, The Stories of My Life, Delhi, Macmillan, 1974.

Dubey, S.N., Indian Political Thinkers, Delhi, Books N Books.

Dumont, L., Home Hierarchicus, Oxford University Press.

Engineer, Asghar Ali (ed.), Communal Riots in Post Independence India, Hyderabad, Sangam Books India (Pvt.) Ltd., 1984.

Gopal, Ram, Lokamanya Tilak : A Biography, Bombay, Asia Publishing House, 1956.

Ganesh & Co. (Publishers), Life of Bal Gangadhar Tilak.

Gellner, E., Nation and Nationalism, Oxford, Basil Blackwell, 1983.

————, Thought and Change, London, Weidenfeld and Nicholson, 1964.

Gupta, Nagendranath, Indian Nationalism, Bombay, Hind Kitabs Limited.

Gunnar, Myrdal, The Challenge of World Poverty, London, Penguin, 1970.

Heimsath, Charles H., Indian Nationalism and Hindu Social Reforms, Bombay, Oxford University Press, 1964.

Haithcox, John P., Communalism and Nationalism, Bombay, Oxford University Press 1971.

Inamdar, N.R. (ed.), Political Thought and Leadership of Tilak, New Delhi. Concept Publishing Company, 1988.

Jog, N.G., Lokamanya Bal Gangadhar Tilak, Govt. of India, Publication Division.

Joshi, V.C. (ed.), Lajpat Rai : Autobiographical Writings, Jullundhar, University Publishers, 1965.

Karmarkar, D.P., Bal Gangadhar Tilak : A Study, Bombay, Popular Book Depot, 1956.

Karandikar, S.L., Lokamanya Bal Gangadhar Tilak, Poona, Sadashiv Peth, 1957.

Kelkar, N.C., Landmarks in Lokamanya's Life, Madras, S. Ganeshan, 1924.

Kothari, Rajni, Politics - India, Delhi, Orient Longman, 1970.

Kohn, Hans, A History of Nationalism in East, London, George Routledge and Sons Ltd., 1921.

———, The Idea of Nationalism, New Delhi, Macmillan, 1944.

———, The age of Nationalism, New York, Harper, 1962.

Murthy, K. Sachidananda, Indian Foreign Policy, Calcutta, Scientific Book Agency.

Munck, Ronald, The Difficult Dialogue: Marxism and Nationalism, Delhi, Oxford University Press.

Muller, F. Max, India: What Can It Teach Us? Delhi, Munshiram Manoharlal, 1961.

Nevinson, H.W., The New Spirit in India, London and New York, Harper and Brothers, 1908.

National Bureau (Publishers), A step in the Steamer.

Neteson & Co. (Publishers), Life of Bal Gangadhar Tilak.

Parvate, T.V., Bal Gangadhar Tilak, Ahmedabad, Navajivan Publishing House.

Pal, B.C., Indian Nationalism: Its Principles and Personalities, Madras, S.R. Murthy & Co., 1918.

Pradhan, G.P. and Bhagwat, A.K., Lokamanya Tilak, A Biography, Bombay, Jaico Publishing House, 1959.

Pradhan, R.G., India's Struggle for Swaraj, Madras, G.A. Neteson & Co.

Publication Division, Govt. of India (Publishers), Trial of Tilak.

Prasad, Rajendra, Autobiography, Bombay, Asia Publishing House, 1957.

Reisner, I.M. and Goldberg, N.M. (eds.), Tilak and the Struggle for Indian Freedom, New Delhi, People's Publishing House, 1966.

Ramakant and Upreti, B.C. (eds.), Nation-Building in South Asia, New Delhi, South Asian Publisher, 1990.

Rolland, R., Mahatma Gandhi, Agra, S.L. Agrawal.
Shay, Theodore L., The Legacy of the Lokamanya, Bombay, Oxford University Press, 1956.
Seer, D., The Political Economy of Nationalism, Oxford University Press, 1983.
Smith, A., Theories of Nationalism, London, Duckworth, 1983.
Tilak, Bal Gangadhar, Gita Rahasya, Poona, Tilak Mandir.
————, The Arctic Home in the Vedas, Poona, Messrs. Tilak Bros.
————, Writings and Speeches, Madras, Ganesh & Co.
————, Speeches of Bal Gangadhar Tilak, Madras, Thirumalai & Co.
————, Samagra Lokamanya, Poona, Kesari Prakashan.
————, Speeches and Writings, Madras, Natesan & Co.
Tahmakar, D.V., Lokamanya Tilak, London, John Murray, 1956.
Tagore, Rabindranath, Nationalism, London, Macmillan Co. Ltd., 1919.
Varma, V.P., The Life and Philosophy of Lokamanya Tilak, Agra, Lakshmi Narain Agarwal.
V. Ramaswamy Shastrulu & Sons (Publishers), All about Lokamanya Tilak.
Wolpert, Stanles A., Tilak and Gokhale, Berkeley, University of California Press, 1962.
William Bentom (Publisher), 1943-1973, The New Encyclopaedia Britannica, Vol. VII.

Journals

The Time of India, Navabharat Times, Hindustan, The Indian Express, Janasatta, India Today and Saptahik Hindustan.

Film

India's Rajiv: A Film by Simi Garewal.

Index